LIVING FREEMASONRY

A BETTER PATH TO TRAVEL

BY MICHAEL R. POLL

A Cornerstone Book

Living Freemasonry
A Better Path to Travel
by Michael R. Poll

A Cornerstone Book
Published by Cornerstone Book Publishers
Copyright © 2021 by Michael R. Poll

All rights reserved under International and Pan-American Copyright Conventions. No part of this book may be reproduced in any manner without permission in writing from the copyright holder, except by a reviewer, who may quote brief passages in a review.

Cornerstone Book Publishers
New Orleans, LA
www.cornerstonepublishers.com
1cornerstonebooks@gmail.com

First Cornerstone Edition – 2021

ISBN: 978-1-887560-95-5

Table of Contents

Introduction vii
Personalizing Masonic Symbolism.. 1
Learning From A Broken Leg.. 9
The Anxiety of Presiding 13
Albert Pike's Morals and Dogma —
   the Art of Communications 17
Symbolism of the Craft Degrees 31
Freemasonry and the Separation of Church and State............ 39
Masonic Meditation and the Rhythm of the Sounds 51
Just Checking in to See How you are Doing, Brother............. 61
Masonic Obligations and the Pandemic 65
Alchemy and Freemasonry 75
Masonic Book Sellers and Publishers —
   the Good, the Bad, and the Unreadable............................ 79
Masonic Memory Work and Elephants 95
Bigotry in Freemasonry... 101
The Two Wolves and Three Bad Guys 111
Vouching for Someone — Yes or No 117
Capt. Kirk Goes to Space — Now You Do Something! 125
The Theory of Stupidity 129
The Importance of Quality Leadership.................................. 141
A Whole Wide World of Masonic Memories......................... 145
The Rewards and Risks of Masonic Education 151
About The Author.. 163

INTRODUCTION

Yesterday, I decided that today I would take a long walk in a nearby park. It's a very peaceful park and feels perfect when I want to relax my mind. Last night, I put out my walking shoes and felt good about the upcoming day. This morning, I woke up, looked outside, and found that it was pouring down raining. I put the news on, and they said that it would be raining most of the day. So, what was I to do?

I poured out my morning coffee and went to sit outside on my covered patio. The rain was rhythmic and the sight of the rain along with the sound was as relaxing as anything I have experienced. I enjoyed the time drinking my coffee. I was not at all disappointed in the change of plans.

The world and everything in it is changing. Freemasonry is facing new challenges. How will we deal with them? Will we rage at things that have changed our plans? Will we be paralyzed in confusion by the changes? I hope not. I hope that we can all find a nice place where we can relax while fate takes us wherever we are to go.

No one controls our minds. We are in control — unless we give up that control. We can't choose or know what will happen tomorrow, but we can choose how we will respond. We can use the many lessons of Freemasonry as a guide for personal betterment — a guide for living better in society. By putting the teachings to use, we can be wiser, more honorable, and happier humans. It's all our choice.

This is a very personal book for me. I've tried to share private thoughts, feelings, and experiences with the goal of contributing to a collective body of possible aid for the seeking Freemason. My hope is that what is offered is of some little help to any in need. All that is offered in this book is offered with the sincere desire to be of some service.

Please accept this work in the spirit that it is given. The goal is always brotherhood.

Michael R. Poll
November, 2021

LIVING FREEMASONRY

Personalizing Masonic Symbolism

One of the things that I've always enjoyed about Freemasonry is its use of symbolism in Masonic education. I appreciate how we use more or less common items to represent a complex thought or object lesson. I know, of course, that the use of symbols is far older than Freemasonry. The use of symbolism as an educational tool can be traced back to the earliest days of man.

But what I like about how we use symbolism in today's Freemasonry is that we can almost personalize it to fit our own needs. Since a symbol is essentially a memory aid, we can take significant past personal events and turn them into our own unique symbols for various Masonic teachings.

Let me give you an example by retelling a nasty event in my life that I use when I want to think of various Masonic moral lessons.

I joined Freemasonry when I was 21. When I was in my late 20s, I decided that I wanted to move to California. So, I did. I moved to the small town of Clovis. It was a nice place to live, not far from the incredible beauty of Yosemite, and also not far from the California coast — places like Carmel and Monterey. There was even a Masonic lodge in Clovis that I would visit on a semiregular basis. It was a good time. But then something very unexpected happened.

One Saturday morning, I was drinking my morning coffee and looking at the newspaper. I saw an ad for an electronics store that was in a shopping center not far from me. I had my eye on some stereo speakers, and now they were on sale for a very good price. I decided to jump in the car and go buy them.

I had about $120 cash on me. I drove to the shopping center and pulled into the parking lot. It was about 10 or 10:30 in the morning. I parked the car and got out. As I was walking to the back of the car, I saw something. There was a kid standing there behind the car. He looked about sixteen or seventeen. As I looked closer at him, I noticed that he had a gun in his hand. I was not exactly happy about seeing this gun pointing at me, but I guess I was having trouble processing what I was seeing. I froze where I stood.

After what seemed to be an eternity (but was probably no more than a couple of seconds), the kid said, "I'll take your money." Everything was brought quickly into reality. I'm not exactly sure what I was thinking, but I didn't have a lot of money, and I really wanted to buy those speakers. I did not want to give him my money, so, I told him that I didn't have anything on me. He cocked the gun.

The gun was a revolver, and I could see the cylinder turning as the gun was being cocked. The barrel seemed to get larger as I looked at it. It started to look like he was pointing a cannon at me. I remember thinking to myself, "What's wrong with you? **Don't play around with him. Just give him what he wants!"**

I told him "OK," then I reached in my pocket, and handed him the money. He took it and just stared at me. I looked in his eyes, and they were just ... empty. There was no emotion, no expression — nothing. They were blank, dead eyes.

Then he said, "You shouldn't have lied to me." I remember a cold feeling coming over me and my thinking, "Oh God, this kid is going to shoot me." I felt helpless. He just stared at me with an odd half-grin.

All kinds of thoughts crossed my mind, and nothing added up. I had no idea how I ended up in this situation. Then, just when I expected to be shot, I saw his eyes dart to his left — right over my right shoulder. A look of shock came over his face. He spun around and was gone. He didn't say a word. He just took off running.

I was stunned, and my first thought was "Police!" I turned around, fully expecting to see a police car or cops running up on foot. But there was nothing. I looked all around. I saw no cars or people anywhere behind me. The closest building was a bank that was towards the end of the mostly empty parking lot, but no one was anywhere around.

I was completely confused and quite shaken. I have no idea why he took off running like he did. I have no idea if he saw someone who took off themselves or what happened. All I did know was that I was very lucky to be alive.

I went home, and "what if?" was all that I could think about. I did a lot of thinking about my life, where I was, where I wanted to go, and how quickly all that I had planned for the years ahead could have ended. Yeah, I did a lot of thinking.

It was clear that I was given a second chance. A few days later, I realized that the lodge in town was having a meeting. I decided to go visit them. I had missed the last few meetings and just wanted to be in a Masonic atmosphere.

Having no idea what was on the evening's schedule, I showed up. As it turns out, the lodge had scheduled a Master Mason degree. I was, needless to say, moved and affected by what I saw in the first and especially the second section.

While the lessons taught in the Master Mason degree focus, in part, on integrity or the test of integrity, my own situation involved no such "test." It was an armed robbery — nothing more. But it made me think a great deal about life itself.

Every single one of us will one day die. We have no choice in this matter. We also have no idea when that day will come. All over the world there are many people who were alive yesterday, planning for their future, and who are not with us today. We will never know what lost plans they may have had for today.

While we have no power over death, there are things that we can do in life.

Until the time of our death, we have total control over our own actions. When that kid had his gun pointed at me, it seemed that he was in control of me. But really, he wasn't. I realized that the money that I had in my pocket was not worth dying for, and I made the choice to give it to him. There was no loss of integrity in my action. I had not given my word that I would not give anyone the money unless certain conditions were met. But what if I had? Then it would have been a matter of integrity. I would have had to very quickly decide if my life was worth my integrity.

That was the test in the Master Mason degree. It was realized by Hiram that we all live and die. It was realized that no one can take our integrity. We are the only ones who can give away our integrity or keep it. It is a powerful lesson. It calls for uncompromising self-examination and unyielding resolve.

But the lessons of that degree involve more than integrity. The overall lessons involve choices that we make and *when* we make them. We have the freedom to go down any life path that we choose. In fact, if we choose one path and at some point, decide that it is not the right path for us, we can choose another direction. We can do this again and again all the way up until the moment of our death.

But when we die, we become locked in whatever path we were on. There is no going back and doing things over or better. The lesson here is to think and choose well. Some choices may be our last.

Another lesson would seem to be responsibilities — the ones we have to ourselves and others. Believe me, if you are under the impression that it is your duty in Freemasonry to gain or maintain power, glory, titles, and degrees (or to prop up those who do believe this), then you are most definitely on the wrong path. We are not about trying to impress others with any "VIP degree or office." The goal of Freemasonry is to take a good man and give him the tools by which he can improve himself. We are to learn and grow. We grow by improving our mind, skills, and morality.

But why do we do that?

I mean, it's a nice idea, but is that all there is to Freemasonry? I don't believe it is. We have a far deeper responsibility. Masonry is not all about us. We must learn how to help others. We are not in this world alone.

A good man, however, can't wave his hand and *make* others good. We can only change ourselves. We have no ability to make others do what we want of them. We can only control *our* actions. What we can do is learn, live, and radiate the lessons of Freemasonry. We can't force anyone down any life path, but we can be an inspiration to others. We can be that guy who inspires others to move to a different, better path — if they choose to do so. We can do that.

We have a responsibility to ourselves and the world to help others as we can. Unfortunately, there is a catch. We can make all the most wonderful plans in the world for next year, next month, or even tomorrow. But, if tonight is our last night on this Earth, then all our good plans are wasted. The lesson is that if we want to do something, we need to do it *now* because tomorrow may never come.

In music, we may know all the proper notes to play. But if our timing is off, then the music will not sound as it should. Timing truly is everything. In all of life, timing is everything. It's not enough to know the right thing to do. We must do it, and we have to do it at the right time.

If we don't care, then nothing matters. But if we do care, then we must accept the reality, responsibility, and the choices in life. Doing the right thing tomorrow may result in being forever known as the guy who refused to do the right thing. All action should be taken now. But, as in all things, the choice is ours.

Learning From A Broken Leg

Some years ago, I was visiting a lodge when I saw something that has probably been repeated often in the whole of Masonry. Before the lodge meeting, everyone was gathered downstairs in the dining hall. I noticed a young Mason in deep conversation with an older Past Master of the lodge. It was a very animated conversation, but as I was a distance away, I had no idea what was being said. The smiling older Brother was clearly instructing the young Mason in something. When I finished my meal, I walked towards the area where they were standing to throw away some trash. It seemed that their discussion was coming to an end. I saw the young brother shake the hand of the older Mason thanking him for whatever he was saying.

It was then that I saw the older Mason's face change from smiling to a look of seriousness. I heard him say to the young Mason, "Listen, you have my phone number. Please call me if you ever need anything at all. We can talk on the phone, go out for a coffee, anything. I mean it. Call me if you need anything." In just that, I saw the heart of Freemasonry and, really, all of humanity. We help each other.

I read something recently about a question that was asked by a student of noted anthropologist Margaret Mead. She was asked if we could pinpoint when civilization (as we normally define it) actually began. Mead said that civilization can be said to have begun with the discovery of a very old human thighbone which had been broken and healed. She pointed out that if a wild animal breaks a leg bone, that's it. The result is death. The animal can't hunt for food or run from other animals. Predators see that the animal is injured and know that it is an easy meal. No wild animal survives long enough with a broken leg bone for it to heal.

A leg bone that is healed means that care by others was given to the one injured. He was not left on his own to die. He was brought into the group and helped through recovery. This, Mead pointed to as the birth of human civilization. It is when we think of the "other" or "us" and not just the "me." It is when we recognize that when we care for one in need, it is caring for us all. This is the heart and soul of the philosophy and teachings of Freemasonry. We care for those in need.

A wild animal thinks only of his own personal needs. He lives and dies by his instincts and skills. An injury to one of his kind means only (to his "me only" mind) that there may be less competition for any available food. No help is given to an injured member of his group. He is left to die. But, when we help one who is in need, it increases our chances of being helped ourselves when *we* become in need. The group as a whole become better protected and stronger. More healthy members of our group means that more food can be gathered for all. Working together was seen to be the most successful way for group survival. The phrase, "one for all and all for one" became corrupted when it was understood as only a pledge to help the king. Its deeper meaning was always to help whoever is weak and then help will be assured for all.

In our most basics teachings of Freemasonry, we learn the importance of helping others. We learn early on that it is not all about the "me." We promise to help others. We see it in our rituals, in our teachings, and in our philosophy. It is a basic part of who we are as Freemasons. We are not to turn away those in need. Period.

I don't know what was being said in the conversation between that young Mason and the older one. But I did see Freemasonry in action. I did not hear the older Mason say that he would help the young brother if he had time or place any conditions on him. He just told him to call, and he would be there. That's civilized human beings. That's Freemasonry. We help each other.

The Anxiety of Presiding

I well remember the first time that I sat in the East (it's now over 40 years ago). I was comfortable in my knowledge of the ritual, but it felt as if everyone in the lodge was looking right at me, just waiting for some mistake. When I was sitting in any other station, I never felt as I did in the East. I spoke my part or did my duty and that was it. I also never pre-judged the Worshipful Master or sat with my eyes fixed on him ready to pounce on any possible error. In retelling this feeling to older Past Masters, I was assured that most everyone feels as if they are under a microscope when serving in the hot seat. I was given assurance that my feelings were not warranted (but common), and that the lodge was supportive and committed to my success. But sitting up there was still a very unnerving and odd feeling.

As my year went on, I grew more comfortable in the East, but I was never far from the anxiety of presiding. I felt the responsibility of the position. I was not only accountable for my actions, but I felt that my actions would reflect on every Mason who sat in that chair before me. I felt humbled. I knew that I would either preside in a manner to bring honor to the station and those before me, or I would not. I wanted to preside well. I saw many others presiding in lodges and other Masonic bodies. It was always the same. You could see the pressure in their eyes. They were aware that what they were doing was either worthy or unworthy of the chair in which they were sitting. Yes, I have seen some who were clearly unworthy of their office. Their unworthiness was recognized by all who saw them in action. But most cared about their actions and wanted to do well.

Over the years, I have seen many presiding officers in many bodies. The most valuable ones know that they hold their office not only when sitting in their chair, but 24 hours a day. What they say and do, even far away from the body over which they preside, reflects on that body. They *are* the presiding officer no matter if they are actually presiding or not. In a world today where we see so much attention on personal rights, it should be made clear that rights and responsibilities go hand in hand. A presiding officer needs to understand that just because he *can* do something does not mean that he always *should* do it. How any Mason (especially one in leadership) acts outside of Masonry will often be understood by non-Masons as the nature of Freemasonry. We should try to be one who is respected inside and outside of the lodge.

If you are in line to be Worshipful Master (or the presiding officer of any Masonic body), please keep a few things in mind. First and foremost, learn the ritual work that is needed for the office and dress accordingly. A Worshipful Master who does not know his ritual or is dressed like he just came to lodge from working outside, will project an attitude of not caring. If you don't care, they won't care. Be familiar with the laws, rules, and regulations of not only the body over which you are presiding but your Grand Lodge. You should be familiar with the history of your body and any particular customs that are important to the membership. Even if you are shaking on the inside, you need to project an attitude of calm confidence. This sort of outward attitude can only come with practice. Do not preside unprepared. Your agenda for the year should have been made when you were early on as a Warden. Practice, practice, practice. Know what events are planned. Know what events can happen at any time (like degrees) and visit other lodges or bodies. Know what others do so that you can learn from innovative ideas (or mistakes) that you may see.

The bottom line is that presiding over any body of Freemasonry is significant. You are not just filling a slot, and you should never consider the presiding officer as one who is just a figurehead. What you do and say matters. A figurehead does not matter. Be dynamic, not timid. Act with intelligent courage. You must show that you care deeply about your office and all of Masonry.

And, of course, don't forget to smile.

Albert Pike's Morals and Dogma — The Art of Communications

When I joined the Scottish Rite, I was given a copy of *Clausen's Commentaries on Morals and Dogma*. I found that book of great value. They had stopped giving out *Morals and Dogma* a few years before I joined. But I found value in Clausen's book.

As I have said many times before, joining the Scottish Rite was like coming home for me. It was exactly what I was looking for in Masonry. I could see the lessons of honor, integrity, duty, service, and so much more. I wanted to learn everything that I could about this system.

I didn't know anything about Albert Pike or *Morals and Dogma*, but because of the title of the book that I was given, it made me ask. I was told that *Morals and Dogma* used to be given to all new members of the Southern Jurisdiction. But they stopped giving it out, (at least, as I was told) because "no one ever read it." I found that to be an extremely odd answer. Why would no one want to read it? They gave the book out to *all* new members for about a hundred years. Why would they give out that many of these books if no one read it? It made no sense to me. That answer made me want to obtain a copy even more.

After a while, I did find a copy of *Morals and Dogma* in a used bookstore. It was a big book, and I could see rather quickly that the style in which it was written made it a difficult read. But I didn't spend that much time thinking about *why* it was written as it was written. I just took the book at face value.

I could see that *Morals and Dogma* contained some valuable information. But I could also see that it was not an actual handbook of the Scottish Rite degrees. I couldn't take the book, and directly, or easily, apply it to that much of what I saw in the Scottish Rite.

The book seemed to be an unconnected, if still allied, commentary on the degrees. I didn't know if the writing style was due to the time in which it was written or just the writing style of Albert Pike. I also felt that the book was more of a secondary source of instruction. I suspected that it might serve me better if I first studied the Scottish Rite and then took the time to delve into this clearly complex book. No one I knew seemed to be able to guide me in this matter, so I just put it aside for a few years.

Since I was in New Orleans and this was my source of information on the philosophy of the Scottish Rite, it was impossible to avoid the history of the Louisiana Scottish Rite in my studies. And, as to that history, I was amazed, shocked, and deeply disappointed at how some (inside and outside of Louisiana) could take what I saw as a pure philosophy and so … corrupt it.

The examples that I saw of out-of-control ego, hunger for power, and pretty much everything that the Scottish Rite stood against was in full display by the U.S. Scottish Rite Masons of the mid 1800's. I wasn't prepared for that, and it did deeply affect me.

My study of the philosophy of the Scottish Rite began to merge with the history of the Louisiana Scottish Rite. It was around this time that I found a few letters that made me pull out my copy of *Morals and Dogma*.

I found several letters written by Albert Pike to his superiors during the Civil War. What struck me right off was that the letters were clear as a bell. What was being said in the letters was not as important to me as *how* it was being said.

I had to pull out *Morals and Dogma* to see if I had made a mistake in my evaluation of his writing style. But I did not make a mistake. *Morals and Dogma* was written in a very distinct style that was very different from these letters that Pike had written to his superiors.

Pike was not only a Masonic philosopher, but he was also a skilled communicator who was able to adjust his manner of writing based on his audience. I found this fascinating and wanted to understand more of the man.

I remember taking an English class in college that was very different from other courses. I was majoring in communications, and this was an English class with a focus on communications. I learned a lot in this class about the art of communication and how we are either bound by our language or we use it as a tool.

Humans who desire to use communication as a tool, communicate on various levels and styles depending on their goals. Humans, like all animals, can communicate on a very basic level. Animals have certain sounds that they make if they see some sort of danger or if they want to announce that they see something important. Humans have a far more complex language and ability to use that language.

A more complex form of communication is when we tailor our words (spoken or written) to achieve certain results.

In times of trouble, humans are not limited to yelling out, "Danger!" We can explain the nature of the danger and what someone needs to do to avoid it. We can use different words to achieve different objectives.

We can make a person look this way, or that way, or do whatever we want all by our selection of the words that we use. We can make things very complex or very simple. If, for example, we want to give directions to someone, we can make the directions very clear and basic. We can give only the information necessary but leave no doubt as to how they should travel to get where they want to go. But, if our goal is to impress the other with how much we know of the area, then we can include many different sites that will be seen on the trip. This won't change the directions, but it will show our great familiarity of the route and the area. Language gives us this flexibility.

One method of giving directions may be self-serving, designed to impress the other with what we know of the area. Another method of giving directions is just trying to help in as simple and clear a manner as possible. If we want to say something, we can make it simple or complicated. And that brings us back to *Morals and Dogma*.

Why did Pike write *Morals and Dogma* and, why did he write it in the way it was written?

Well, we can't get into the head of someone who has been dead for pushing 150 years. But, if we look at the time and the situation, we can see that the Southern Jurisdiction wanted to reorganize and rebuild itself in the mid 1800's. Prior to his becoming Grand Commander, Pike had been appointed to a Committee to reorganize the Southern Jurisdiction rituals which were in a debatable state — from near non-existent to disorganized following some twenty or more years of inactivity and then limited activity.

A book explaining the degrees would seem of obvious value. But *Morals and Dogma* is not just "a book." What was the purpose of this book?

The job of a communicator is to take something (information, ideas, etc.) from one person and present it to others, like the information contained in a book. Pike took complex philosophical discussions and presented them in a book tied to the philosophy of the Scottish Rite.

It's true that Pike took generous portions from various esoteric authors and included them in his work. But it would be a mistake to think that Pike did not write the majority of the book. Even when we look at the sections written by others, it was Pike who organized, edited, and placed them where he wanted.

Albert Pike was clearly a very intelligent and gifted man. By just looking at *Morals and Dogma* and the letters that he wrote during the Civil War, it's obvious that he was capable of adjusting the style of his writing depending on his audience.

It's understandable why Pike chose a very clear and easy to understand style when writing to his superiors during the Civil War. He wanted no confusion or question about anything that he was writing. But why would he choose what can be fairly called an obscure writing style for *Morals and*

Dogma? Was being perfectly understood his goal, or could his goal have been something very different?

As mentioned earlier, we can't get into Pike's head or ask him questions today about his writing style. But there are only so many options as to why he structured and wrote *Morals and Dogma* as he did.

It is possible that Pike believed that anyone who had achieved the 32nd degree in the Scottish Rite had received sufficient education in esoteric matters to understand his manner of writing.

So, let's look at that theory a little closer.

The man who introduced Pike to the Scottish Rite was Albert Mackey. Mackey was an educated man who wrote a number of well-respected Masonic Books. He even wrote a classic Masonic encyclopedia. Mackey was certainly able to understand the writing style of *Morals and Dogma*.

Pike's Scottish Rite instructors were in New Orleans. Individuals like Charles Laffon de Labebat, Claude Samory and others in the New Orleans Scottish Rite leadership were also clearly able to understand Pike's manner of writing. But, what about the rank and file Southern Jurisdiction 32nd degree Masons? What about the ones who had not yet received the 32nd degree? What type of Scottish Rite education did they receive? It's hard to say.

It's not exactly clear how much Scottish Rite education the average 32nd received in the mid to late 1800's or how much time was normally spent before receiving the degrees.

Available records vary as to the time and depth of the education.

We might want to say that a good deal of time was spent on education but proving that may be difficult. A series of interesting events, however, took place following the Civil War (right around the time that *Morals and Dogma* was being published) that should be examined.

From its creation until just before the time of Pike, the Active Members of the Southern Jurisdiction, meaning the 33rds, were all from Charleston, South Carolina. Yes, some did move away from time to time, but 33rds were selected from the Charleston area in the early years.

The Active Membership was also limited to nine members and the office of Sovereign Grand Inspector General was tied to the 33rd degree. In other words, when you received the 33rd degree, you were also made an Active Member of the Supreme Council — an SGIG. This was changed in the Southern Jurisdiction just before Pike received his 33rd degree.

Albert Pike was one of the first 32nds who was elevated to the 33rd degree who was *not* at the same time made a SGIG. He was one of the first of what is today known as a "white cap" — that is a 33rd who is not a voting member of a supreme council. Pike received his 33rd in 1857 and became Grand Commander in 1859.

Following the Civil War, Pike realized that if the Southern Jurisdiction was going to survive, it had to expand and grow. He did some remarkable things. For one thing, he expanded the number of Active Members from 9 to 33.

Pike then made a serious push to expand the Scottish Rite to all areas of the US where there was no Scottish Rite. To do this, he made a smart decision. He focused on Grand Lodges.

There was no limit at that time on how many "white caps" could be created, so Pike started giving out the 33rd degree almost like awards. Grand Masters, Past Grand Masters, Grand Lodge Officers, and such with no prior experience in the Scottish Rite were made "white caps" and in payment for this "award," they would talk up the benefits of joining the Scottish Rite in their state.

It worked. The Scottish Rite did start to grow in all areas of the US. The Southern Jurisdiction did expand.

Individuals with some ability and who did the most work for the Scottish Rite were awarded with Active

Membership in the Southern Jurisdiction. But there were consequences created from this manner of growth.

Individuals were awarded with degrees and honors for what they did or could do *for* the Scottish Rite, not for what they knew or learned *of* the Scottish Rite. As such, many started becoming the Scottish Rite leaders, but they knew little to nothing about the actual Scottish Rite philosophy.

So, in an environment where the leaders, the teachers, knew next to nothing of the Ancient and Accepted Scottish Rite, what could they teach the new members? Not much more than ways to get honors and leadership positions. It became an educational trap.

To grow, the Scottish Rite needed movers and shakers. It needed Grand Lodge leaders. But many of them did not take the time to learn the deeper aspects of the Scottish Rite. Many did, however, have considerable experience in how to manage organizations and get others to join. These talents became key for the Scottish Rite growth.

Morals and Dogma became a book that might as well have been filled with blank pages. Because the philosophy in the pages of the book was unknown and unread by far too many in the Scottish Rite leadership, it was unknown and unread by most all of the membership. The operational blueprint seemed to be finding ways to assure that money was in the bank, get new members, find ways for them to attend meetings, and train them for leadership in this organization. That's it.

Doing the day-to-day business was commonly seen as the real duty of the Scottish Rite Mason. The goal was not to join, learn, and live the philosophy of the Scottish Rite. This may explain why *Morals and Dogma* became the most owned yet unread book of the Scottish Rite. It was held up high as that massive book of the Scottish Rite that can be read by any with the time and interest. But so very few made the time necessary to read it.

And why should they spend so much time and effort to read such a difficult book? You could get "honors" and leadership positions by just pleasing those in leadership. And, after all, the leaders probably didn't read it either.

But then again, maybe Pike only drafted the book to impress or intimidate those in the Southern Jurisdiction hierarchy. Maybe by writing the book as he did, those in the leadership might say that Pike was the obvious choice for leading the Southern Jurisdiction through those challenging times. He *had* to be very smart to just have authored the book!

Maybe Pike wrote the book with no intention of it being an actual teaching tool, and its only use was to be a resume of sorts for getting to the top of the Scottish Rite. Again, that's only a theory but a darker theory.

The truth is that I don't know why Albert Pike wrote *Morals and Dogma* in the manner that he wrote it. I may have thoughts, but they are only thoughts. It's clear that Pike wrote it in that style by choice. But *why* is a matter of debate.

The fact is that what is inside *Morals and Dogma* has not been a major influence for many of the Southern Jurisdiction

Scottish Rite Masons. If he wrote the book with the belief that all 32^{nds} would have received sufficient Scottish Rite education to appreciate and understand the book, he was mistaken.

I believe that it is perfectly fair to say that *Morals and Dogma* has been more of a mascot than an actual Scottish Rite education tool for most of the time that the book has existed. But times have been slowly changing. Over the years, there has been a recognition by some that Scottish Rite education is exactly what is needed to advance the Scottish Rite. Yes, some still consider a valley to be successful if they merely have a successful recruitment campaign, but a change is taking place.

The Scottish Rite Research Society was created in 1991. We cannot and must not minimize the work that this organization has done for quality Scottish Rite education. It's publication, *Heredom*, has on its own, been of tremendous educational value to the whole of the Scottish Rite.

In 1995, Cornerstone Book Publishers began a program of publishing classic and new Scottish Rite Educational books. The goal was to get valuable, long out of print educational works out to the memberships. Cornerstone focused on not only Scottish Rite education, but research into its early history. I can assure you that I faced considerable disapproval by some in Scottish Rite leadership who felt that this work was not only unnecessary but unwanted.

In 2003, the Scottish Rite Valley of Guthrie, Oklahoma, established the College of the Consistory. This was an actual Scottish Rite school designed for the education of Scottish Rite Masons. The work done by the Valley of Guthrie as well as its driving force, Illustrious Brothers Jim Tresner and Robert Davis, needs to be seen as a major step towards a real, organized, and structured Scottish Rite education program.

In 2009, the Southern Jurisdiction's Master Craftsman program opened its doors. With the College of the Consistory as a model, the Master Craftsman Program offered quality Scottish Rite education in a near classroom setting. Reading material would be mailed to its students and then testing would be done to assure an understanding of the lessons provided. The driving forces behind this program included Illustrious Brothers S. Brent Morris and Arturo de Hoyos.

In recent years, the NMJ opened its "Hauts Grades Academy" proving serious Scottish Rite education. And the Southern Jurisdiction has revived and reopened the Masonic Book Club providing quality Masonic educational books.

Much is happening and there is reason to expect much more. Yes, we still have some in various local and regional leadership positions who may not exactly enjoy this wave of education. Ego, pride, arrogance, etc., all can still be found in too many areas that make life difficult for too many hungry young Scottish Rite Masons.

The good news is that many in leadership positions today recognize the need for genuine Scottish Rite education. The work of educating new members is taking place in more and more areas. New Scottish Rite Masons are learning what it means to be Scottish Rite Masons. Yes, changes are taking place.

As for *Morals and Dogma*, yes it can be a most difficult reading experience. But it is not a waste of time. The book contains extremely important esoteric and philosophical truths woven into the Scottish Rite theme. And for an even more rewarding reading experience, I would recommend Arturo de Hoyos' *Albert Pike's Morals and Dogma Annotated Edition*. This extraordinary work takes the classic *Morals and Dogma*, and both somewhat modernizes it and explains much of what was behind the words of Pike. I highly recommend this book for any student of the Scottish Rite.

Anyway, that's my thoughts on *Morals and Dogma*. I don't have an answer as to why the book was written as it was written, but I also don't believe it is very important. The book should not be looked at as a Scottish Rite handbook, but as a supplement to not only the Scottish Rite, but to Masonry and esoteric societies of all flavors. It is a book that should be used, and not one just sitting on your bookshelf.

Symbolism of the Craft Degrees

I'D like to explore a few aspects of the Craft Degrees in Freemasonry. I'd like to try and look at how and why we do certain things — and how things may have changed from the very early days of the Operative Freemasons.

Today's craft lodge has three degrees — the Entered Apprentice, Fellowcraft, and Master Mason. In fact, or through inspiration, Freemasonry has grown out of the old Operative Freemasons — the builders of the great cathedrals of the Middle Ages.

In the days of the old Operative Masons, a young boy who showed promise, and who was found to be honest and worthy, was taken in by a Master craftsman and would serve about seven years as an apprentice. He was essentially a helper and would learn all aspects of the building trade taught to him by his master.

When the Master felt that his apprentice had learned all that he could be taught, and his work was judged to be acceptable, he would be given something of a test.

The apprentice would be asked to complete a "Masterpiece." This would be some piece of work that would represent the skill and ability of the apprentice. If he passed this trial, he would be accepted into the guild as a *Fellow of the Craft*. This meant that he was a full member of the guild and able to earn wages like any other member.

The idea of degrees in Masonry may not have existed in the time of the old Operatives. In the early Manuscripts of Operative Masonry, we see only mention of *Apprentices, Fellows,* and *lodge officers*. The degrees seem to have been developed in the 1700's. The lodges formed themselves and evolved into what we have today as a three-degree craft lodge system.

When we look at our degrees today, they can be confusing and often open for misinterpretation. Things that we do, things that we expect of the candidates, and even many of the words that we use can be … problematic. They seem to be of a different time. That's because it's true. They *are* of a different time. Many of our words and practices come from hundreds of years ago. Let's look at some of our practices and what they may actually mean.

Freemasonry presents many of its lessons by means of symbolism. A symbol is simply one thing that is used to represent something else. A sign on a building with a piano can be used to quickly show that this is a music store that sells pianos. In the early days of Operative Freemasonry, many to most of the people couldn't read. An inn might have an image of a mug of ale, or a bed, or something else helpful rather than spelling out the word *inn*.

The symbols that we use in Freemasonry make sense when we think about the work of the old Operatives. The symbols represent various aspects of Operative Freemasonry. And yet, we can assign to them additional meanings having to do with morality, human character development, and good-will. Nothing in any symbol or teaching of Freemasonry teaches or suggests anything other than morality and assisting the candidate to become a more useful member of society.

Let's talk now about one of the most misunderstood and questioned aspects of Freemasonry — the Obligation. What does it mean, and why do we need it?

But first, we need to recognize something. For nearly as long as Speculative Freemasonry has existed, there have been anti-Masons. Freemasonry is, frankly, one of the most attractive targets for conspiracy theory. Anti-Masons love to claim that we seek to take over the world, possess vast riches, and guard over all the world's wealth by means of horrible *blood oaths* that we extract from unsuspecting candidates.

I really don't know how many times I have sat around a dinner table at lodges with Masons who were laughing about such nonsense. "Where's *my* share?" "Why did they leave *me* out of all the riches??" It is nonsense born out of ignorance of Freemasonry and a failure to think out the situation. But some do choose to believe in unicorns.

Operative Freemasonry worked under strict rules and laws. Guilds, fraternities, and other such organizations had more or less standard forms of oaths or obligations which were approved by both the crown and the Church. They were basically, "do this" and "don't do this." The actual penalties for violating any of the obligations of the Operatives were the same then as they are today in Speculative Freemasonry. The actual penalties consisted of reprimand, fines, suspension, or expulsion. That's it. They were and are few and simple. Any capital penalties then or now would violate civil and religious laws.

In the Middle Ages, lodges of Operative Freemasons existed at the will and pleasure of both the crown and the Church. If these lodges had written *anything* into their obligations which violated any law or rule, and acted on them, they would have been disbanded and arrested.

But symbolism has always played a part in all aspects of Freemasonry. We also must remember that to be just expelled from a lodge of Operative Freemasons in the Middle Ages could have meant an actual death sentence to an Operative Mason. Working was how they put food on the table for themselves and their family. They needed to work to live. To be expelled would likely mean they could no longer feed themselves. They would also be excluded from the actual physical protection of the group and alone they would face the dangers of the harsh and often cruel Medieval world. It was a dangerous and harsh time. Today, expulsion from Freemasonry means only that you can no longer enjoy being a Freemason. Life was different in the Middle Ages.

One of the most recognized symbols of Freemasonry is the Square and compasses. These were implements used by Operative Freemasons. The Masonic apron is another well recognized symbol of Freemasonry. A white leather apron was more than a method for an old Operative to protect his clothing and carry his working tools. The apron has symbolic meanings worthy of study.

The white leather apron, while today being mostly white cloth aprons, is said to be an emblem of innocence and the badge of a Mason. This means that Masons are taught to live by a moral code of conduct. Masons who refuse to live within our moral code or who violate the laws of their community can be expelled.

The Masonic apron also denotes Masonic rank and office, not only within the lodge, but also within the district or Grand Lodge.

Speculative Freemasons today, by far, do not work in the actual building trade. Some may be actual stone masons by profession, but it is certainly not required. In our lodges, we don't use the Working Tools of Freemasons as they were originally intended. For example, the 24-inch gage was another Operative working tool, but for us today, it is a symbol of proper time management. It teaches us to recognize the need to use our time on Earth to serve the Almighty, help our fellow man, and in ways that help us grow into better human beings.

The common gavel was an actual working tool and is a symbol for us to chip off the rough edges in our character and moral development. On our altars is the Holy Bible, which is the rule and guide to our faith and practices. Many of our lessons and teachings come directly from the Bible. While our doors are open to worthy men from all faiths and practices, it is the symbolic lessons from within the Bible where we draw the teachings for our candidates.

The Square is also one of the actual working tools of the Operatives. But in our Speculative Masonry, it is one of our many symbols from which we teach moral lessons. The square is also the insignia of the office of Worshipful Master. In addition, it has also worked its way into our common language. We speak of a "square deal" with the meaning that it was a fair or honest deal. Other Masonic symbols, words, and practices have also worked themselves into our culture and language.

If you are a new Mason, or one who has, or is, thinking about petitioning, or even an experienced Mason, please listen for a minute. The goal of the old Operatives when taking in an apprentice was simple. They wanted to teach him all that they knew so that he would become a highly skilled worker who would bring honor, respect, and work to their guild. Our goal as Speculative Freemasons is to take in candidates, and by means of moral, symbolic lessons, have them become better human beings and more valued members of society.

It is strongly suggested that your Masonic Monitor, Law Book, and other educational materials available from your Grand Lodge and other sources, be studied well. Unlike those who did not learn their work in the days of the Operatives, no one will expel you from Speculative Freemasonry for failing to learn our symbolic lessons.

But I can tell you that if you spend time and learn what is offered in the EA degree, as well as those that follow, you will have a richer and far more rewarding life. Freemasonry will not force anything on you. But you do not become "better" by only joining and paying your dues. It takes work, dedication, and a desire to improve yourself.

Freemasonry can open the door for you, but you will be the one required to decide if you walk in or stay on the outside.

FREEMASONRY AND THE SEPARATION OF CHURCH AND STATE

There is a phrase that I often see that has always fascinated me. It's, "Separation of Church and State." This phrase is often used when discussing political and religious practices in the United States government. But it also can apply to aspects of Masonic tradition and philosophy. But what does the phrase mean? I believe that we should examine the history of the phrase, along with how we sometimes understand its meaning and origin. I'd also like to look at problems that have developed over the years from debated interpretations of the phrase. Such a study can contribute to a healthier appreciation of how and why Freemasons use the philosophy of this phrase in our teachings and practices.

To begin with, prior to the American Revolution, religion for those living in the thirteen colonies was dictated by the laws of England. England, like most all European countries, had a state religion and the citizens were required by law to profess whatever religion was approved by the government. Those who professed other religions could be fined, imprisoned or even, in some cases, put to death for the "crime" of having a religious faith different from what the government allowed. Now, the people living in the American colonies were considered citizens of England and were bound to its laws. As time passed, they became increasingly upset at being told what they could and could not believe.

A question that quickly comes to mind about laws attempting to dictate religious beliefs is how do you actually control what someone else believes? Well, you can't. No one can read someone else's mind. You can, by law and punishment, control what people *tell you* that they believe. But, you can't make a law requiring that all of your citizens switch to a religion of your choice and also expect that others will change how they believe in their hearts. All that you can reasonably expect is that the people will tell you one thing but likely continue to believe whatever they want. When you think about it, this type of law existing anywhere is the perfect recipe for a very disgruntled population.

Religious freedom was not the only demand of the early American colonists, but it was an important one. The people wanted the freedom to openly believe and belong to whatever faith they chose. They did not want the government to tell them to which religion they must belong or how and what they should believe. That was too personal of a decision for anyone but the individual to make. But a great mistake is to believe that the colonists wanted a government void of any and all mention of religion or the moral teachings of religion.

The belief in God is written into all aspects of the Constitution and early documents of the young United States government. But, what about this separation of church and state? Wasn't that written into the Declaration of Independence or Constitution? No, it was not.

The seeds for the concept of separation of church and state can be traced to an 1802 letter written by President Thomas Jefferson to the Danbury Baptist Association in Connecticut. This letter was read by many when it was published in a Massachusetts newspaper. The Danbury Baptist Association were a group of Baptists who were concerned because they were a minority religion, and they feared that the government would take control of them, forcing them to change their nature to better match those of the majority faiths.

President Jefferson wrote:

"Believing with you that religion is a matter which lies solely between Man & his God, that he owes account to none other for his faith or his worship, that the legitimate powers of government reach actions only, & not opinions, I contemplate with sovereign reverence that act of the whole American people which declared that their legislature should 'make no law respecting an establishment of religion, or prohibiting the free exercise thereof,' thus building a wall of separation between Church & State."[1]

Now, a problem with words is that their meaning may not always be completely clear. This is why we should try to understand the environment in which words were written or spoken. In this case, Jefferson wrote this not too many years after the creation of the United States which fought a war, in part, to attain religious freedoms. Jefferson is saying that the United States was not in the business of creating a state religion and that all citizens were free to worship as they felt best. The government was not going to tell anyone how they should worship. This was the private and personal choice of everyone.

This is the same view that Freemasonry has of religion. To start with, Freemasonry is not itself a religion. It has no desire to tell anyone how to worship, provide its members with any path for salvation, or tell anyone that this faith is better than another faith. That is a private matter between each Mason and God — by whatever name the Mason uses to define the Supreme Being. Masonry does not involve itself in the particulars of a member's religious faith. All that we say is that we should recognize that there is something greater than us, and that we should worship however our heart dictates. We teach our members about living as best as they can during their lifetime and that each member should look to his own religion and its teachings for matters concerning the afterlife.

Sometimes, problems develop when someone says "A, B, & C" and then someone else, many years later, comes along and asks what was meant by "A, B, & C." If the one who originally said it is no longer alive, then all that we can do is try to give an answer using our best reasoning as to the meaning. We may be right, or we could be a little or a good bit off. There is also the matter of individual free will. For example, just because we say that the government will not favor one religion over another, can we point to any aspects of the government which may have done just that?

Let's use a 3rd grade public school teacher in our example. Let's say that she is a woman of deep religious faith. She truly and deeply believes in the teachings of her faith. She also has the opportunity to educate and mold an entire classroom of young minds. She cares about these children. She begins introducing and then teaching the qualities of her own religious faith. She even, at times, represents it as the *one true faith*. This is what she believes, and she certainly does not believe that she is doing anything but helping the children.

This teacher is placing her own faith above the faith of others. She is not a politician nor an elected official in any local, state, or federal government. She is a teacher in a public school. But as such, she does represent an important aspect of government. She is a figure of educational authority who uses that position to advance her own religious beliefs above others. She does so in a classroom of young children with impressionable minds. That's a significant position.

This teacher may well believe that she is doing what is best for the children under her care. She has, however, compromised the balance that was intended to exist between providing a basic, nonspecific foundation of religion and advancing one's own faith over another. Anyone who has read anything about Thomas Jefferson knows that this is exactly the opposite of what he meant. This is just an example, but it is what began happening in many public schools by many teachers throughout the 1800's and into the 1900's.

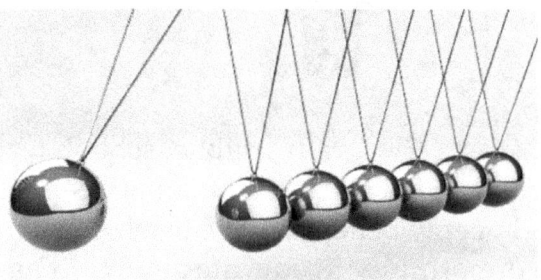

Balance is a tricky thing. If you represent balance with a pendulum, then you can see that if you pull the little ball out of the center balance position and then let it swing back, it swings first out of balance in the other direction. It will then swing back and forth in both directions before eventually finding the center balance position. You pulled it out of balance in one direction, but when you tried to correct it, it swung out of balance in the other direction. This will happen every time. There is a message here.

The founding fathers knew exactly what they meant in regard to the policies that they created. But over time, they died, and questions would come up that needed clarification. One question that repeatedly seemed to come up concerned this concept of "separation" between the church and state. Did this separation mean that all forms of government were to be void of any aspect of religion? Well, that answer was always a quick "no." Most all early U.S. documents reference God. Prayer was in all branches of government. It is very clear that the general foundation of religion was in all aspects of government. The particulars of religious faith, however, were left up to the individuals. Unfortunately, and maybe most notably in the area of public schools, this led to abuse and the pulling of the pendulum out of balance.

School teachers were entrusted with the education of young minds. It is a great responsibility and requires dedication and care on the part of the educators. There was a balance, a tightrope, which needed to be walked. On one hand, prayer with basic religion and morality were taught to all students. The idea was to give a religious or moral foundation which could then be built upon by the students with the house of worship of their choice teaching the individual religious lessons. Of course, it was also perfectly acceptable if one chose to have no religion at all in his life. The government was not going to tell others how to believe or if they should have any religious beliefs at all. The schools simply laid out the basic path from which the individuals could travel wherever they chose. On the other hand, was the religious beliefs of the teachers.

As long as the teachers did not take that extra step into the area of specific religious teachings, it was felt that all would be well. Teachers were expected to shelve their own personal beliefs and not step over the line into advancing their own religious convictions to the impressionable minds of their students. Regrettably, the failure of teachers who felt the uncontrollable need to advance their own personal beliefs in schools became common. It was not just Christianity that was advanced, but specific, and many times different, branches of Christianity that were taught to students. Parents were not happy when they saw their children influenced by religious teachings that they felt should be taught in houses of worship, not public schools.

In 1947, a case known as *Everson v. Board of Education* went to the Supreme Court. In his majority opinion, Justice Hugo Black wrote: "In the words of Thomas Jefferson, the clause against establishment of religion by law was intended to erect a wall of separation between church and state." Notice the words, "was intended." Justice Black was interpreting the meaning of Jefferson's words. This interpretation helped lay the foundation for the near removal of all mention and aspects of religion from not only public schools, but many to most branches of government. The "wall of separation" became understood to mean, "religion over here" and "government over there.' The two could not mix.

Because of past abuses and attempts at influencing public school children regarding religious beliefs, the attempt at correcting the abuses resulted in the pendulum effect. The pulling the ball out of balance by the influencing of children in matters of religion resulted in the attempt to correct this situation by the supreme court. The ball of balance was released from its out of balance position, but instead of returning to its center position of balance, it went out of balance in the opposite direction. Instead of a situation where the government (or any aspect of it, such as public schools) would not attempt to dictate or influence its citizens in regard to particular religious faiths, they moved to a position where religion would be purged from just about all aspects of government.

But where does Freemasonry stand? Well, the position of Freemasonry is very clear in its many written and verbal teachings. Freemasonry is not a religion. It does not influence its members to accept any religious beliefs over others. We do not evaluate the worth of a candidate based on his religious faith. A belief in a Supreme Being is required in all regular lodges in the United States, but we do not dictate particular religious beliefs.

But, just as all aspects of Freemasonry mirror society, so does this situation. Little by little, religious abuses have been taking place. There have been cases, and it is growing, where membership into Freemasonry has been influenced by the religion of the candidate. If one is a member of "the wrong religion" then they may not even receive an application, much less pass a ballot. Lack of proper Masonic education has resulted in more than a few starting to believe that membership into Freemasonry is limited, or should be limited, to Christians. In addition, some view the word "Christian" as only applying to specific branches of Christianity. Ignorance of Freemasonry is putting us on a most dangerous path.

It is far too late to put out a cry to better guard the West Gate. Far too many with limited actual understanding of the teachings of Freemasonry have entered all levels of leadership in Grand Lodges, the York Rite, and the Scottish Rite. To deny this does not help us. Like a swinging pendulum, the laws of nature must be obeyed. When we go too far out of balance in one direction, then we end up swinging back too far the other way. Time is the only remedy. Patience and wisdom are the only salves that we can apply to weather the challenging times that may be ahead.

The good news is that we can see young Masons all over working hard to advance Masonic education through educational gatherings, teaching events, and publications. This kind of education must continue. It is not a quick fix, but it is a sound one. We must support others when we see them trying to do the real work of Freemasonry. Yes, where Masonic knowledge should exist, ego and/or ignorance still control too many in leadership. Be patient with them. Help them where you can. Walk rather than battle. We must not stop learning and passing on what we have learned. Be assured that it will take time, but it is the work that must be done if we hope to see the Scottish Rite as it should be.

The phrase "separation of church and state" has different meanings to different people. It is not the intent of this paper to provide political opinions as to actions taken by any branch of government. Looking at the world through the lens of Freemasonry is the goal. Freemasonry does not favor any particular religion over another. We judge the moral worth of the individual. Period. Likewise, individual Masons should not judge others seeking to join, or those already in Masonry, by their religious faith. During our history we have had many highly respected and influential Masons of nearly every imaginable religious faith. Each was judged by their Masonic work, not by their religious faith.

We need to pay attention to ourselves and our own growth in Masonry as well as humanity. We need to work towards balance in all aspects of our lives. We also need to recognize when things are out of balance and not expect unreasonably quick corrections. We need to have patience, be dedicated, and allow wisdom to guide our thoughts and actions. We need to govern ourselves accordingly.

NOTES

1. Jefferson, Thomas. Jefferson's Letter to the Danbury Baptists: The Final Letter, as Sent. The Library of Congress Information Bulletin: June 1998. Lib. of Cong., June 1998. Web. Aug 7, 2010,.

Masonic Meditation and the Rhythm of the Sounds

Maybe we can look a bit at meditation in this paper — but from a little different angle. I'd like to discuss some of the classic ideas of meditation, but also touch on other meditative practices — even writing with meditation in mind.

The idea is to look at a rhythm within us that can help us live life to its fullest. Understanding this rhythm is what I believe to be the foundation of humans finding the balance between ourselves and all around us. It has been my experience that meditation, in all its forms, is one of the best tools to helping us discover true harmony between ourselves and our universe.

Now, before we start, I don't mean to suggest by the title of this paper that meditation practices are unique to Freemasonry or that Freemasonry has some sort of personalized meditation ceremonies. In fact, there are not a great number of Masonic lodges that use meditation in their lodges. It should also be said that many Masons have little to no information about meditation. In addition, some of those who *have* heard of it do not always embrace the idea of meditation, especially in lodges.

But I'd also like to talk just a bit about the word "meditation" as the word itself may mislead some who may actually be helped by it. And I was one of them.

Words have always meant something to me beyond their obvious meanings. At first, I didn't connect any of this with meditation. Meditation was pretty much unknown to me. I knew the word "meditation" but not much of how it applied to living. A lot of what I did was done simply by instinct and a natural inclination to go on my own with things. For example, when I write, I have always tried to choose words and sentences that follows a beat that runs in my head. I've never known why. It's just something that I've always remembered doing. If pushed, I imagine that it has something to do with the relationship between sound and music.

Music follows a rhythm which seems to be based on the beating of the heart. When music, or any sound, connects with someone, it can affect their emotions. It can calm, excite, or have any number of effects on the individual. Music, or certain sounds (including words), can be used in meditation. In fact, some books can be meditative just by the way they are written.

Music, spoken words, and sounds in general, create vibrations that can be felt by people even if they are unaware of it. We are instinctively drawn to vibrations that are in tune with us and repelled by those which are not. The words that I choose when I write depend on the subtle flow of the sentences — meaning the natural, and hopefully unnoticed, rhythm of the words. I'll use "and" or "or" quite a bit if it helps the beat of a sentence. And by "beat," I mean the rhythm of the sentence, the way it flows and sounds in your head when you say it.

I'll also be generous with descriptive words, and I don't always mean adjectives. I will normally add these words in a series of three with the goal of extending or completing a rhythmic count. Even the number of syllables in a word is important, as they may throw off, or complete, the beat of any sentence.

Quite often, I count the number of syllables in an entire sentence. I do spend a good deal of time writing and rewriting. The selection of words that I use involve trying, maybe not always successfully, to follow a natural rhythm that flows up and down depending on the mood that I'm trying to convey in what I am writing.

I've had editors in the early days come in and change things that I'd written to make the piece sound, in their experience, more scholarly. I would sometimes spend considerable time trying to create a mood and flow with my word selection, only to find that editors had completely changed the beat and flow to something lacking any natural rhythm. They were technically correct, but it was not where I was going with what I had written. I've gone into this a bit with several earlier papers.

In my early days, I did what I did naturally without much thought of "meditative writing." My first book was published in my late teens (early 1970's). It was a collection of poetry, or prose, and song lyrics. Oddly, if you had told me several years before I wrote the book that this would be the type of writing that I would first publish, I would have laughed. I had a complete misunderstanding of poetry. I was a teenager and concerned with being and looking "cool." Poetry did not, in any way, seem *cool,* and I had no use for it.

But then I read two books that pretty much changed everything for me. The first was *Listen to the Warm* by Rod McKuen and the second was Kahlil Gibran's *The Prophet.* These books were considered poetry, but they were completely unlike what I had experienced in my limited reading of the subject. They were not "mushy" or childish rhymes, as I viewed poetry. They were thoughts, feelings, and philosophy. Communications, and my understanding of it, changed forever and a new world opened for me.

Reading these books actually relaxed me and made me look deep within myself. This was a type of meditative writing. I realized that *this* was the type of writing that I was doing all the while, and I had just never realized that I was doing it.

The reason that I have been going into my initial misunderstanding of poetry and writing in general ties in with a confusion I had of meditation itself. I didn't know much about meditation and certainly did not realize that one could meditate while reading. I also did not know that certain styles of writing lent themselves more towards meditation. Unfortunately, my first exposure to meditation started off on the wrong foot. And I do mean that literally.

My first experience with meditation came when I enrolled in a class in Transcendental Meditation. I was in my late teens or early 20's. The class was held in an old area of New Orleans known as the warehouse district. It was in a very old building, and we had to take a shaky freight elevator to get up to the classroom. The instructor looked like a ragged, old hippie (of course, I looked like a young one) who had not bathed in some time. He had a crazy look in his eyes, and for most of the class, he just sat on the floor crossed-legged and barefoot, playing with his toes. I was not impressed. I was so distracted by this guy that I couldn't pay attention to anything that he said. I never went back and dismissed meditation as nonsense.

I judged mediation based on him. That was my mistake. The funny thing was that during this same time I often did something very similar that helped me with my writing. I just didn't connect the dots.

I often found that by doing something that I called "zoning out," I would have an easier time writing. I would sit somewhere and just clear my mind of all the garbage that I had picked up during the day. When I did this, I could begin to see what I needed to do or write.

This was all when I was in college. I remember one day sitting under a tree on the campus "zoning out" when something odd happened. While I was sitting there, someone came up behind me and said, "Hi Mike." It startled me, and I turned around to see who was there. They realized what happened and said, "Oh, I'm sorry. I didn't realize that you were meditating." That irritated me a bit. I quickly said that I was *not* meditating and that I was only *zoning out*. She looked at me and said, "Ah yea, that's meditating."

I began searching for more information on meditating. I didn't want to become involved with any person or group who had ideas about meditation similar to the guy I had experienced in my teens. I joined the Rosicrucian Order and found there a peace in their manner of education. Meditation was a part of their instructions.

I also sought out others who provided additional information on meditation. Increasingly, I saw the value in this form of "zoning out." I learned that while many have their own ideas as to what is the best or most successful method of meditating, it's most useful when you find what works for you rather than just copying whatever the other guy is doing. What works for one person may, or may not, work for another.

And really, it doesn't matter if you call it meditating, or zoning out, or eating candy apples. What you call it doesn't matter. But, if names are important, and you are a bit uneasy about the word *meditating* as you have heard that "strange people" do it, try calling it ... "relaxing." We all like to relax.

If you would like to try meditating, or relaxing, it's really simple and doesn't take much time and certainly no effort.

So, to start, find a place to sit down. It can be a chair, the floor, or anywhere that's comfortable. Set a timer for maybe 5 or 10 minutes to start. You don't need to do this for lengthy periods of time to benefit from it.

Sit in any position that is comfortable for you. Some people find that placing their hands in their lap works, or really, any comfortable position. It's all up to you.

Close your eyes, and just try to focus on your breathing. Don't force or change anything, just pay attention to the rhythm of your natural breathing. Try to keep all your attention only on your breathing.

If your attention is pulled away by a loud car passing by outside or any noise that you may hear, it's OK. It's also OK if your mind wanders to any thought that pops in your head. The goal is not perfection. The goal is just to clear your mind as much as possible, relax, and come to recognize that internal rhythm within you.

Don't be hard on yourself, and don't expect perfection. Just try. No reasonable person expects to start exercising and after five minutes to have a perfectly toned body. Start slow and be kind to yourself.

Some people meditate daily, and others find that once a week works best for them. It's up to you. But routine is good. Pick a time to meditate that normally does not interfere with other things. If you feel that once a week is best, pick a day that is normally open, say Thursday, or *whenever*, but stick to the time that you set.

Think of long term rather than short term. If you expect too much too quickly, you can become disappointed and quit. If you only seek to relax, and clear your mind of the daily grind, that would be a perfect beginner goal.

I like to think of meditation as a means to help put ourselves in balance with all around us. If you think about it, most of the time we go around with our daily lives almost on auto-pilot. We pay little to no attention to the trees, birds, animals, or anything other than the next meeting that we need to attend or something that we need to pick up at some store.

Meditation is a means to help connect us with ourselves and all around us. It is not a cure-all, but a means to help restore balance to our lives. It is a working tool that we can use if we choose.

If it does not work for you for any reason, well, you tried. Maybe another time will give you better results. Pressure should never be applied to meditate or to not meditate. But, if you are interested in meditating and find value in it, don't listen to someone who is telling you that you are wasting your time. You're not.

Please understand that this paper is only a *very* basic introduction into meditation. I have not gone into things like music, incense, candles, or many other things that help some, and are less helpful to others. I'm allergic to incense and never, ever use it unless I feel the need for a massive headache. But find what works and is helpful to you.

If something in this paper has touched something in you to dig a bit deeper into meditation, then seek out answers. Those who sincerely seek answers will find them. The world is better connected than we may realize.

Just Checking In To See How You Are Doing, Brother

I'D like to talk a little today about an old tradition in Freemasonry that many times seems to have gone by the wayside — and I think that's unfortunate.

Nearly every day, I am contacted by Masons asking questions about some aspect of the Scottish Rite or Masonry in general. But then, not long ago, I was contacted by a brother with a message that surprised me. He wasn't asking anything, he simply wrote, "Good Morning, just wanted to say "hi" and check in to see how you are doing."

I was stunned. I just don't get these kinds of messages very often. It took me back to the days when this was common in Freemasonry. I had forgotten that this is how Masons and lodges used to operate. We would check in on each other to see how we were doing. If we didn't see a brother in a while, we would call him or go visit him to see how things were going. Lodges sometimes had committees or set members who would check in on members who had been absent from the lodge. It was not to reprimand them for not showing up at lodge It was just to check in on them to see how they were doing and let them know that the lodge was thinking about them. Sadly, sometimes we would contact a brother to learn that they had fallen sick or some very hard times. By learning of their situation, we would be better able to render whatever help we could for the brother.

But there is an attitude that I have noticed growing over the years that I find is getting in the way of Masons and lodges reaching out to their brothers. It is an attitude that has almost evolved unnoticed. It seems to have to do with a feeling of self-importance that is growing in the hearts of too many. It is the "I'm the one who is important" attitude — "You are going to come to me."

I once overheard a brother say that if a Mason gets sick or falls in need, then he should let the lodge know, or he should not expect the lodge to help him. He then said, "You can't expect the lodge to go chasing after all the brothers who don't care enough about their lodge to even show up or call the lodge to let everyone know how they are doing."

What a backwards concept of Freemasonry! And we wonder why some lodges are having so much trouble with revolving door membership.

It would be very easy to move this discussion to one of pointing out the misinformation and lack of Masonic knowledge of some Masons, but I'd rather take another direction. I'd rather focus on what we should do, rather than on what we are not doing or doing wrong.

Simply put, regardless of what anyone else is or is not doing, we need to reach out and check on our brothers. We need to check in on those who we do not see often to find out about their welfare. We need to take the extra step without any judgement and with only brotherly concern and care in our hearts and minds.

Today, it is very easy to reach out to others. Most everyone today has a cell phone on them or close by. If you can't reach someone on your phone, you can leave a voice message. You can also send an email or text to the brothers that they can read whenever they find it. There are many ways that you can reach out to others that is not intrusive yet very effective.

At times, our world seems divided and angry. But we are Freemasons. We do have a higher calling. When someone petitions our lodge, we evaluate them and judge their basic moral worth to see if they can be one of us. After that time, they are one of us and due the extra steps and time that we should give those who we care about.

We care for our brothers. We treat them with respect. It does not matter if they are young or old, if they are new members or 50-year members. We respect them.

A way to show respect is to reach out to one who has been away to just see how they are doing. We reach out because we care. Try doing something without spending a lot of time on the details. Take a moment right now and send an email or text to a brother you have not seen or heard from in some time. Just tell him that you have been thinking about him and wanted to check in on him to see how he is doing. Don't ask questions about why he has not been around, just ask how he is doing.

I promise you that just that simple act will brighten his day — even if he does not openly acknowledge it. It means something to everyone for someone else to unexpectedly inquire about their well-being. But don't stop there. After you have done this, contact another brother.

Just take a couple of minutes from each day and shoot off emails or texts to those who you have not seen around lately. Send simple messages letting your brothers know that you are thinking about them and hope that all is well with them.

But again, don't stop even with these contacts. Report your activity to your lodge at your next meeting. Let them know what you have been doing and the results. That may inspire others to do the same thing. That's Masonry. That's doing what we all should be doing. Don't make excuses, just do it.

Masonic Obligations and the Pandemic

Not long ago I was invited to attend a Zoom online gathering for a lodge event. That event was to discuss my book, *The Particular Nature of Freemasons.* The lodge members wanted to ask questions about various things written in the book.

One question has stuck with me, and I have been debating the question over and over in my mind. The question concerned a paper in the book on the COVID-19 pandemic. I'd like to take a deeper look at this question.

To start with, the book was published in May of 2020. This was in the very early days of the pandemic. I noted in the paper that I wore a mask when I went out (and still do). My feeling was then, as it is now, that it seems to be such a very little thing to do, and if it is at all possible that it helps, then why not?

I also noted how many seemed to be so very put out and upset by being asked to do most anything to help with the pandemic, from wearing masks, to staying out of crowds — anything. Some seemed to be just angry at everyone. It seemed that whatever was asked to be done, or not to do, was flat-out rejected by a good many people.

A sizable portion of our population seemed to want to do exactly the opposite of whatever the medical community advised us to do. Clearly, the feeling was that the doctors at the CDC and elsewhere either didn't know what they were talking about or for some reason were lying to everyone. As unbelievable as it is, the pandemic became a political football. Truth became subjective.

The question the brother asked was if I felt today, given everything that has happened, that Masons were "obligated" to be vaccinated as we promise to care for our brothers. Well, that's a hot button question. I did a lot of thinking about it, and I feel that I should share my opinion.

I pointed out that so very much has changed since that paper was written. We now have a vaccine, and a booster has just been approved to extend the protection of the vaccine. That's the good news.

The bad news is that we have a new strain of this virus, the Delta strain, and it has been running rampant. We also have close to 800,000 in the US alone dead from this virus. That is certainly considerably more than in May of 2020. In addition, we still have a good many of the population who deny that the virus is real, refuse the vaccine, and reject wearing masks. The claims for these objections are that they question the quality of the vaccine; they demand freedom to do as they like; they do not trust the government or medical community to tell them the truth; they believe it is all some grand conspiracy to take away our freedoms, and many other claims.

So, what is the truth? Is the vaccine working or not working? And does Freemasonry play any role here?

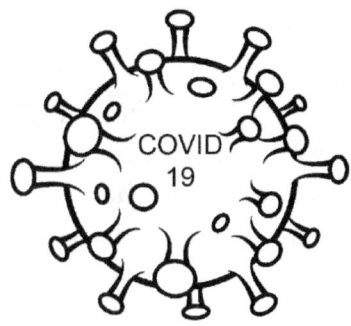

At present, and this is July of 2021, some 99% of the recent COVID deaths in the US are among the unvaccinated and those who are not fully vaccinated.[1] I believe that it is clear that the vaccine does the job that it was created to do. We are even starting to see a backlash of anger against the unvaccinated.

Hospital emergency rooms are often filled with extremely ill, *unvaccinated* COVID-19 patients. Heart attacks, cancer, and many other non-COVID emergencies are not able to always get help in emergency rooms because they are filled with unvaccinated COVID patients.

Many see the unvaccinated as bringing all of this on themselves by their refusal to be vaccinated. Many feel that they should not be allowed to take up needed hospital beds for something that can be seen as their own fault.

Well, we can't do that. We don't refuse needed medical treatment to, say, drug addicts who overdose. Sure, we know that a claim can be made that many drug addicts have done this to themselves, and so have the unvaccinated. We don't deny anyone medical attention because of self-inflicted harm. Civilized societies don't act that way.

We care for all our citizens — the responsible and the irresponsible ones. This attitude of, "I'm out for me and the devil with you" is not how civilizations grow. It's how they die.

And then there is this overlaying and interwoven divisiveness and often blind, raging anger that is seen far too often — on all sides. If someone says something that you don't agree with, then they are the enemy and in need of being destroyed.

Everyone is mad at, and points to, the other guy as the source of all the problems. Opinions are presented as facts, and facts are understood by whatever someone believes. In too many cases, truth becomes defined by whoever has the better debating skills. It was when I saw someone online post that they do not have to wear a mask or get vaccinated because "God will protect them," that I saw a deeper aspect to this situation.

Some view the "truth" of the pandemic as they view religion. We don't have to prove religious beliefs by science. We accept religious teachings because we choose to believe them. We have faith because we have faith.

I've seen many COVID studies saying one thing, but a single contrary opinion touted as *the truth* by some. Evidence becomes selective and only accepted if it agrees with a preconceived opinion. Some see any challenge to their COVID belief as a challenge to their religion. These people will not allow anything to deny them of what they believe about any aspect of COVID.

Of course, there is another group that simply loves to debate and argue. They will never admit to a mistake or to being wrong. They will withhold anything that does not support their argument and doggedly maintain only what makes them sound correct. They care about winning, not the truth. They want a certain opinion advanced and will skew all information to fit only what will support their position.

And we can't leave out the internet and TV talking heads who gain ratings by the most unbelievable nonsense that traps listeners or viewers. They know that they are spouting falsehoods, but it is what brings in the paycheck. They will change nothing until the ratings start to fall.

And this brings us back to the question of if those Masons who *refuse* the COVID vaccine are violating their Masonic obligations?

Masons are not to harm or do wrong to each other. We know that. But let's say that a Mason is leaving a lodge meeting. He starts to drive off, and all of a sudden, he loses all steering control, and the brakes fail. The car slams into several brothers as they are leaving the lodge. One is badly injured, and the other dies. It was a horrible accident.

Regardless of what the police do or don't do, should the lodge file Masonic charges against him? He was driving a car that hit and injured one brother and killed another. We are obligated not to harm each other.

Well, I believe that it would be difficult to find anyone who would say that charges should be filed against him as it was an accident. He didn't know that the car would lose its steering and brakes. He didn't intend on doing harm to anyone.

But the fact is that this is not the whole, complete story. The truth is that his car was old, and someone told him recently that they heard "funny noises" coming from the car. He was advised by knowledgeable mechanics to have the car checked out as soon as possible.

He denied that anything was wrong with the car and said that it was all nonsense. He didn't *believe* that the car needed repair. While he did not plan or mean to do it, his failure to take proper action with his car seems to be the direct cause of what happened. The same can be said of COVID.

The ones who refuse the vaccine and refuse to even wear masks could be perpetuating this virus. They deny it, but reasonable evidence goes against them. But do we try someone for this?

My family and I are vaccinated. I've read and listened to as much information as possible on both sides of this issue. We chose vaccination as it seems to be the most reasonable path to staying as safe as possible. We know that nothing carries a 100% guarantee. This is the reason that we will take the booster as soon as it is available.

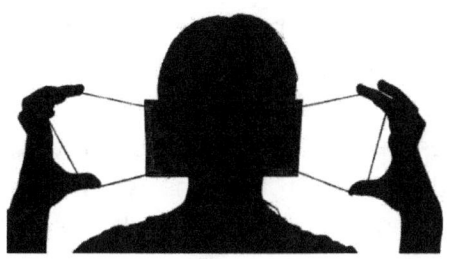

We wear masks when we go out for two reasons. First, it does seem to be at least some additional protection. But the second reason is because we know that break through infections can happen. We know that masks protect the wearer as well as others. We are trying to do our part in keeping this infection as contained as possible. We are trying to be as responsible as possible. But what about the other guy?

Well, it seems that many do not believe that any action by them is necessary. They live their lives as they choose with no regard for others. Do I believe that's Masonic? No, I do not believe that this type of attitude is at all Masonic.

We all have a moral responsibility to protect each other. At least, we must agree that we have a responsibility not to harm each other. I believe that regarding this pandemic, it is irresponsible and against all Masonic teachings to want to, and demand, to just go about our lives as if nothing is going on.

If someone has actual fear about this vaccine, then at least wear a mask. That's such a small thing to ask. The arrogant attitude displayed by many who refuse to do anything that may protect others is not the actions of true Masons. Masons do watch out and care for each other.

But as to what can be done about those who refuse to do anything at all that may help others, well, I don't believe that there is really anything that we can do except try to protect ourselves as much as possible. Unless laws of the land are violated, then I see too many dramatically divided opinions on this subject for any sort of successful Masonic trial for not being vaccinated.

I believe that Masonic trials at this time for being unvaccinated or not wearing a mask would only further divide us all. We do have many who are Masons in name only, and I have written a few papers on why.

If you have concerns about this pandemic, then there are things that you can do that may help reduce the odds of your becoming infected or passing on any infection to others. If you have not been vaccinated, get vaccinated. That's a no-brainer.

*Masonic Obligations
and the Pandemic*

If you have been vaccinated, get the booster when it is available. Wear a mask when around others. Avoid crowds, especially crowded indoor locations. Wash your hands, keep clean, and do the things that you would normally do to stay healthy. Talk to your doctor for medical advice. Listen to your doctor or medical authorities, not the guy down the street, some talking head on TV, or internet nonsense. Be smart, considerate of others, and realize that we are all in this together — even if others don't always realize it.

I wish that I could say something that would cause us to unite as one to beat this pandemic, but I just don't have the words. All that I can do is pray — and I can have my say on this platform.

NOTES:

1. https://medicalpartnership.usg.edu/covid-19-staggering-statistic-98-to-99-of-americans-dying-are-unvaccinated/.,
https://www.cnet.com/health/99-of-covid-deaths-are-now-of-unvaccinated-people-experts-say/.
https://www.businessinsider.com/us-coronavirus-deaths-nearly-all-among-unvaccinated-cdc-head-2021-7

Alchemy and Freemasonry

The subject for today is alchemy in Freemasonry.

The reason I wanted to write this short paper is because of something that I read in an online post not long ago. A Mason asked if anyone could tell him anything about the alchemical aspects in Freemasonry. Another Mason answered his post as follows:

> "Listen carefully, alchemy plays no part whatsoever in Freemasonry. It is a lie created by those ignorant of Freemasonry."

Then he signed his name and below his name in large capital letters, he wrote: *PAST GRAND MASTER*. He didn't say which jurisdiction, just *PAST GRAND MASTER*. I was … pretty unhappy when I saw that post. Let me explain.

In numerous papers I have written on the importance of Masonic education. I've spoken on the dangers of individuals with limited knowledge of Freemasonry reaching leadership positions and then displaying their ignorance of Freemasonry as if ignorance was knowledge and falsehoods were fact.

Please listen for just a moment.

The philosophy of alchemy is the principle of taking something less and through work, making it into something more valuable. The common symbolic representation of this process is the taking of base metal and turning it into gold. That's the "hook," the appealing image that makes others take a second glance.

The actual goal of alchemy is to take a good man and make him better. Ever heard that phrase before? You should have read that phrase in most all Masonic literature that attempts to define Freemasonry. We take a flesh and blood human being who is basically good and through moral instruction, give them the tools to improve themselves. That's Freemasonry. That's alchemy.

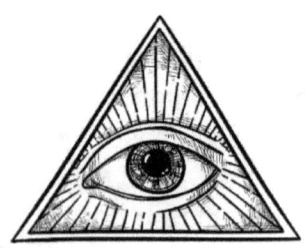

To those who are true Seekers of Light, be on guard. Be careful of answers without explanations. Be cautious with those who use their titles or positions as evidence of knowledge of Freemasonry. Don't be rude, but also don't be taken in by self-professed "authorities."

The Hiramic Legend teaches us that the real danger comes from within. Don't allow those who may have only been in the right place at the right time to lead you down the wrong path. Recognize ego and ignorance when you see it and be on guard.

Masonic Book Sellers and Publishers — The Good, the Bad, and the Unreadable

How about we take a little look at Masonic books? But let's go a bit deeper into the production of books in general as well as sellers who may or may not be doing us a service. I'd like to share my thoughts on how we should evaluate both, so that we can get the most for our money.

First off, let's look at how we get our books and what makes a "quality" book.

I've been a Masonic book publisher for over 30 years now. But prior to that, I worked for many years in the printing industry. I've worked in offset printing, instant printing, and actual letterpress printing. For several years I was employed by the last letterpress shop in New Orleans. I operated small hand letterpresses and the larger automatic presses.

Back in "the day," there were rules as to what could be identified as a *printing press* and what could only, by law, be considered as a *duplicator*. A *printing press* was defined as a letterpress and *only* a letterpress. An offset press was called a *duplicating machine*. There was a very real snobbery in the classification of who was and who was not *real printers* and *real printing presses*.

Hand Letterpress

No such rules or laws exist today as you can only find letterpresses in a few specialty printing shops. The entire industry has changed — actually, several times.

I came into the printing business at the tail-end of a unique time when letterpresses were on their way out, but they still exerted influence on the printing industry.

I'm not going to go into a full history of printing, but only say that in the 1940's and 50's, offset presses were proving to be high quality, fast, and far less demanding to operate than letterpresses. But they were *not* letterpresses and could not call themselves "printing presses."

Letterpress operators dismissed these new presses as cheap imitations of *real printing*. These same offset presses are today the ones so often said to produce "real printing." Times have changed!

A.B. Dick Corp. offset press with chain delivery

Are offset presses good? You bet they're good. So, why were the "real printers" — the letterpress operators — so upset at these new machines?

Simply put, they required a new skill set to operate and put letterpress operators and especially type setters out of work. It was an industry change that was better for the general public and industry, but not so much for the letterpress operators and small print shop owners.

Offset presses used thin metal plates to print (or duplicate) from an original. Large cameras would photograph an original and (using the same method as producing a photograph) develop the plate with the original "burned" into the plate. The metal plate was then attached to the press.

The offset duplicating machine or press would use rubber rollers to carry ink that would roll over the plate covering the plate with ink. Other rollers carrying water with a solution would also roll over the plate, washing off all the ink except in the areas where the text or images were "burned" into the plate.

The plate would then roll over a rubberized cylinder transferring the image there, and that cylinder would roll over the paper transferring the image to the paper. The printed page would then roll into a delivery tray. That was it. No more typesetting using lead type. And they were so much faster than letterpresses!

As for quality, well, that seemed to be subjective and depended on who you asked. Letterpress operators would swear that offset printing was less quality, but offset operators would argue that offset quality was indistinguishable or better. Offset printing ended up replacing letterpress because business owners realized that *if* there was any loss in quality, it was far, far made up by the speed and less difficult to operate offset presses.

In the 60's and 70's, technology continued to develop and companies such as Xerox and IBM came out with new improved photocopy machines. I was working in an offset printing shop when we leased a large commercial copy machine. We had it in the front of the shop as a self-service machine for people who only wanted one or two copies of something.

Around this same time, new developments in offset printing were taking place. New "paper plate" cameras were invented, which were along the same lines as the Polaroid camera. These new cameras with attached developers were showing up in more and more shops, which became known as "instant print" shops.

There was a large flatbed table with a glass on top under which you would place the original. A photo was taken of the document, and a "paper plate" was processed inside the camera. In a few minutes, this one-time use plate would pop out the back of the camera.

A solution was rubbed on the plate, and it would be attached to the press. The printing process would then be the same as with a metal plate, except where a metal plate could produce thousands of copies before the text would deteriorate, a "paper plate" would only be good for under a thousand or so copies. But on short runs of five hundred or less, it was hard to tell the difference.

The offset industry was now divided between "commercial printers" (metal plates) and "instant printers" (paper plates). I worked for a while in a New Orleans "instant print" shop near a few major oil companies. These companies would often want a handful of copies of reports of about ten to twenty pages. They did a *lot* of these reports. It was high profit for the print shop owner.

The problem was that they wanted them very quickly, and they often came to the shop all at once creating a backlog of work. But these jobs did make up a good bit of the company's business.

One day the shop owner had so many small reports to do that he ran a few on the photocopy machine. Bang, just like that the job was done! No messing around with ink, cameras, presses, or anything. And, on top of that, it was as profitable *or more* than when run on the press.

It very quickly became the norm to run small jobs like these on the photocopy machines. This was not, however, a brand-new idea.

In 1970, a small shop was opened near the University of California in Santa Barbara. This shop consisted of only photocopy machines and was targeting college students. The shop was called *Kinko's*. It was a hit. Before long, Kinko's copy shops were opening all over the country.

The idea was simple. If you had something you needed reproduced, bring it to Kinko's, and you can quickly get copies. The good side of this was that you could get copies of most anything quickly, and it was not that expensive.

Sure, it was not the same quality as offset printing, but most of the customers didn't know or care. They wanted copies of their book reports or whatever *now*, and Kinkos could get them copies *now*.

During the 80's and 90's, photocopy technology was also booming. Copy machines were created that could handle most anything from business cards to large maps. The reports that were so profitable (but time consuming) for instant print shops were pieces of cake for Kinko's. Copy machines could collate small reports and staple them together all inside the machine. The printing industry was revolutionized.

It wasn't long before someone wondered if they could reproduce books by using copy machines. The answer was yes!

Early on, stapled, and spiral bound books were created all inside copy machines. Even card covers were added inside the machine. But, what about softcover, perfect bound books? Soon copy machines were created where you could put a manuscript into a feeding tray, and it would be fed into a copy machine and copied. Then the pages of the book would be collated, fed into a conveyer where the edge would be passed over hot binding wax, and then pre-folded covers would be attached.

In one step, a perfect bound, softcover book could be produced. It was quick, cheap, and in your hands before you could blink an eye. It became *popular.* Did it give you a good quality book? Not really. But again, it was quick and cheap.

Around the same time as all of these developments in copying, the internet was starting out. It was not long before this new photocopying technology for books began being advertised on the internet by a new style of book publishing companies.

These new book publishers targeted writers who wanted an easy and cheap way to self-publish their books. Prior to this time, publishing a book was an expensive endeavor. You could not expect to make a cent on a new book before selling many thousands of copies. But, with these new photocopy books, you could buy copies of that family history you always wanted to write for just a few dollars.

The new self-publishers would help you with layout and even cover design. Book sellers also found the internet a wonderful way to sell books, and some large book sellers who did not take advantage of the internet in its very early days soon went out of business. Selling books on the internet became *the* way to sell. Publishing books through these self-publishing companies became *the* way to get books on the market.

Before long, the internet was flooded by self-published books. It was a wonderful time for internet book sellers, and freelance writers, but not so great a time for book buyers. Let me explain.

Photocopy machines work on a very simple process. You put something on the machine to be copied and whatever you put there will be reproduced. Here, an old saying is appropriate — *garbage in, garbage out.*

The copy machine does not care what you give it to copy. It will copy anything. The standards of the book publishing industry dropped dramatically. There are several reasons why these standards dropped.

The first reason is money. Prior to the photocopy, self-publishing technology, book publishing was an expensive business. It cost book publishers a great deal of money to publish a book. Even before a book saw a printing press, large investments were made into copy editing, layout, and cover design. The quality of the writing had to justify the large investment of the publisher.

A standard run for a commercial book publisher could be 100,000 copies of a book. That was often considered a necessary run for any book that hoped to turn an acceptable profit for the publisher. But, for these self-publishing companies, a writer could get a single copy of his book. With little to no investment, a writer could not only get a copy of his book, but he could see it for sale on the internet. Sure, they would have to do the editing, layout, and cover design themself, but these self-publishers made it reasonably easy. Before long, the internet was flooded by self-published books.

At first, it seemed like a good day for the readers. All sorts of new books were on the market, but it soon became something less than enjoyable.

One problem (and simply put) was that the writing of many of the self-published books was far from an acceptable quality. Readers would buy books because they thought the subject might interest them, only to find that it was not much of an enjoyable reading experience. Writing a book doesn't mean that it is a good book. But there were also additional problems.

The photocopy machines that were used in the "copy shops" and self-publishing companies used a process that needs to be understood. When something is printed using any type of printing press, the ink stains the fibers of the paper. The paper is permanently changed. The ink will remain on the paper for as long as the paper exists.

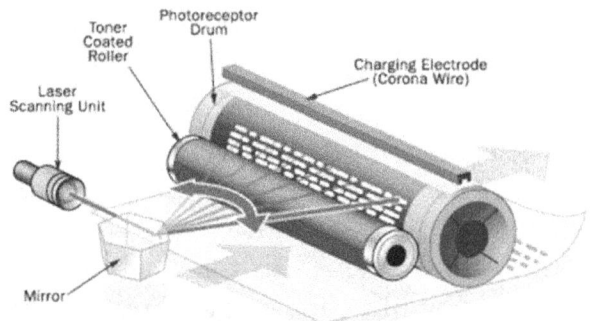

Early photocopy machine process

Early photocopy machines used a powdered toner that was "attached" or "stuck to" the paper by an electric charge that ran though the toner when the paper passed through the machine. When you quickly looked at the paper, it seemed like something that was printed because the images were on the paper. The problem was that this electric charge did not stain the fibers of the paper like ink. The charge simply *bound* the powered toner to the surface of the paper. It was not designed to be there forever.

Early photocopy machines might see the toner — or words — falling off the paper in a matter of months or, at best, a couple of years. For reports that were read and then tossed, it was unimportant. But, for books or anything that you wanted to keep, it was a big problem.

As technology improved, the life span of the words on the paper was extended but for only about 50 years at best. Additionally, if the electric charge was too low or too high, other problems were created.

A charge that was too low would result in a very short "stick time" for the toner or the words. A charge that was too high might result in other problems.

Since the job of the charge was to stick the toner to the paper, if the charge was set too high, it could result in the toner sticking to both sides, resulting in pages sticking together. The all-around quality issues of these photocopy books resulted in very bad reputations for this new industry.

And then there is the matter of Masonic books. I well remember in my early days of Freemasonry being frustrated when I would see lists of recommended Masonic books. I would try to locate the books on these "must have" lists only to discover that most of them were long out of print. I would have to search used bookstores for copies of whatever I sought. Sometimes I would get lucky, but other times I would be left wanting.

But with this new self-publishing movement that was taking place, Freemasonry was not left out. Before long, I started seeing many of these long out of print books available as reprints by photocopy publishing companies. Delighted to see some of the books on my "must buy" list, I bought a few of them. But I was more than disappointed by the quality of the books that arrived.

I paid good money for books that were many times almost unreadable. Four to five pages in a row might be so burned out that I could only see a few letters on the page. Pages would be stuck together or printed almost sideways. The quality was horrible! This was not the type of books that I was used to reading. Sure, I understand that mistakes in printing can happen with any print job. Even with major, well-respected companies, printing errors can happen. But when the replacement copies of the "bad copies" were delivered, the exact same problems existed. These were not printing errors; it was the quality of the originals! It was clear that rare books were grabbed and then quickly scanned with little to no care about quality. I was both angry and exceedingly disappointed.

It was this frustration that gave me the push to use my printing experience to create my own book publishing company. I would sometimes spend weeks cleaning up text from very old Masonic books. Most of the time, no one knew the work that was often involved, and I guess that's the way that it should be.

Today, digital technology, or computer technology, is light-years away from what it was in the early days of photocopy machines. A digital print when compared to an old continuous tone photocopy is almost like talking apples and oranges.

The electrostatic charge process has completely changed, and the problems of toner "falling off the pages" is no longer an issue as in the past. The process used today also *does* stain the paper fibers almost like the process of printing with ink.

When everything is considered, the quality differences today between print on demand digital printing and offset printing are limited to the quality of the writing, layout, and design of the book. I have seen offset printed books that are of far less actual quality than digitally printed books.

So, why do we still have offset printing if digital printing is for all intended purposes of equal quality? Well, cost is a major factor, but it is not the only factor. Many book publishers, small and large, use *both* offset and digital printing, depending on the book or the run number.

For large runs, meaning thousands of copies, offset printing is by far cheaper. As a rule of thumb, the bulk of the cost involved in offset printing comes during the production setup. Once the big presses are up and running, the per book cost is far cheaper than the per book cost of print on demand digital books. But on the other hand, if you want a small number of copies, then print on demand will give you a much smaller overall cost.

Large book publishers today utilize both types of printing depending on the goal of the copies being printed. By that I mean, books designed as promotional or advanced copies will more likely be digital print on demand as they will not require substantial amounts of copies.

When a large publisher releases a major publication with 100,000 or more copies going out, you can be assured that it is offset printed as the cost would be astronomical if they used print on demand technology. As for print quality, they are almost indistinguishable today.

Today, the market for books is wide and many times demanding. Many have firm ideas as to what they want and what will be accepted. Others have no idea or don't care.

Print on demand still often has a stigma from the early days of photocopy books. It's mostly not justified, but it is there. This is one reason many printers and publishers are not completely open about discussing the process used for specific print jobs. The quality will be the same no matter which process is used, but many times if a customer knows that a job will be print on demand, they will, even before seeing it, assume that it is of less quality.

On the other hand, many embrace the innovative technologies of print on demand and realize that not only can the results be of high quality, but publishing opportunities are now open that simply could not be afforded if offset were used. Even letterpress is making a comeback as a specialty printing option. For those who truly love the feel and ownership of a uniquely printed and bound book, there are options. Yes, it costs more, but there are places where you can get quality hand printed and leather-bound hardcover books that look and feel more like works of art. For others, Kindle offers thousands of books that can fit on and be read off small handheld electronic readers. It is today a wide, varied market.

But a warning. Unless you are careful, you may end up paying far more for your book than is necessary. In one place on the internet, you may find a rare reprint, softcover selling for under twenty dollars. In another place, you may find the very same book, and I do mean the *very same book*, selling for almost a thousand dollars. That's right. Buyer beware is alive and well on the internet.

So, for the new Mason who wishes to learn about Freemasonry, what should be done? Well, let's stop for a second and think about why we have books. It's to make communication portable and longer lasting. You can take a book anywhere and read it when you want.

But the book itself is not really what is important, it is what is written in the book that's important. The heart of a book is the message, ideas, or information being given to the reader. Masonic books are of value if you use them, not if they are just room decorations.

There is nothing wrong with beautifully printed Masonic books, but we should not use the cover to judge the book. If you can't find a needed book in gold-leaf hardcover, then get it in paperback or Kindle but get the information.

Used books can be a great way to save money. But you must be careful. Some places sell used books for higher than the retail price of a new copy. Do a little work and find the best prices.

Support Masonic book publishers directly. Most all the time they make far less than you might imagine. But most of all, read and learn.

Masonic Memory Work and Elephants

Recently, I was contacted by a young man who told me that he was in a difficult situation. He said that he had petitioned a lodge and just received notice that he was balloted on and passed the ballot. He said that he was told that he would soon receive his initiation. But it seems that what would follow the initiation is what concerned him.

He said that when the investigation committee visited him, they told him that following each degree, he would need to memorize a catechism and then stand an examination in open lodge. He would need to recite what he memorized. That worried him. He said that he was extremely concerned about this as he did not, at all, like speaking in public and was very bad at doing memory work. He was afraid that he would fail horribly.

I told the young man that the point of the memory work was not to embarrass him or to make sure that we have copies of our ritual. We have printed rituals safely stored away. No one has to worry about that. The point of doing the memory work is to drive home the point that we hold things that we earn as far more important than things that are given as gifts or prizes.

In Freemasonry, we should work for what we receive. The memory work expected of new Masons is not designed to put anyone on the spot, nor is the work expected to be letter perfect. What is expected is that the candidate shows that he worked hard to do what was asked of him.

As to his concerns that he is not up to the job of memory work, I told him to just give it his best shot. Everyone there wants only to help him. I told him that a side benefit of this type of work is that it is mental exercise, and it does, in itself, help everyone.

I told him that the mind is a very powerful tool and can do more for us than we might imagine. The mind can open doors for us by expanding things that we can do, but it can also limit us if we don't use it wisely. A strong mind is our friend. A weak mind is not.

In talking about memory work and the mind, a story that I read years ago concerning memory may be of some value.

One summer, a young boy was visiting India with his family. One of the things that the boy very much looked forward to doing was riding an elephant. So, they went to a place that offered elephant rides.

When he first saw the elephants, he was absolutely awestruck at how incredibly large they were. As he was looking around, however, he noticed that there were no fences keeping them from roaming off. He did see that they were all tied with a rope around their ankle, and the rope was staked to the ground. But even as a boy, he knew that something was wrong with the rope that was being used. It looked very thin for these massive elephants. He didn't understand why they couldn't easily snap the ropes and just walk off.

The boy asked a worker about the ropes. The worker told him that the elephants had been with them since they were first born. As very young elephants, these ropes were strong enough to hold the small animals. They didn't have the strength or size to break the ropes ... at that time.

Now, elephants have good memories, but they don't seem to always use these memories to their best advantage. You see, as adults, they are large enough and strong enough to break the ropes, but they remember being young and how the ropes held them fast. They remember the past and *believe* that the ropes will not break. They believe that these are very strong ropes, so, they don't even bother trying to break free.

The elephants have very good memories, but they don't always apply logic to their memories. They use their memory but not their minds. There is a powerful lesson in their behavior for all of us.

In Masonry, use of the mind is essential to all facets of our teachings. Yes, we are taught the importance of memory, but also of using the mind to our best advantage. We can apply reason, intelligence, and logic to memory. We have the ability to believe that we can or can't do things. Of course, we can believe all day long that we can flap our arms and fly ... but we can't. But there are so many things that we *can* do, if we only believe and apply ourselves.

The Masonic memory work expected of candidates is not busy or nonsense work. It is not designed to make anyone feel inferior. It is work designed to lay a solid foundation for future lessons. These are lessons that we can either take advantage of and grow from, or we can do only the basics and belong to a club.

So, for the young man about to join and worrying about doing the memory work, relax. The members of the lodge are on your side. No one is trying to play games with you. These are your friends and soon to be your brothers.

Freemasonry is not some 2nd rate college fraternity looking to have fun. We are a system of morality, veiled in allegory, and illustrated by symbols. These words do mean something. Soon, you will get to see how and why.

BIGOTRY IN FREEMASONRY

IN the early 1990's, a series of online debates took place which became known as the "CompuServe Anti-Masonic Debates." I took part in these debates. During one debate, an anti-Mason asked me the question, "Does bigotry exist in Freemasonry?" I gave him a straight answer. I told him that bigotry is nowhere in the philosophy or teachings of Freemasonry. But I added that bigotry did exist within the hearts of some Masons who do not understand the teachings of Freemasonry. That started a long back and forth debate as to the actual nature of Freemasonry. I'd like to look at this subject, but like I often find value in doing, I'd like to lead into it from a little different angle.

I remember back when my oldest son was about two or three years old. My wife and I were sitting in the living room watching TV. He was in his room, playing quietly — or so we thought. All of a sudden, we heard a loud bang, and the crashing of glass. We had no idea what was going on but rushed into the bedroom. There, with a look of shock on his face, was my son. He was standing on the bed with a large broom in his hands, and the glass light fixture that was on the ceiling, on the floor in pieces. As soon as we realized that he was OK, I asked him what in the world happened. You could see in his eyes that he was working out the best answer, and then with a look of pure innocence, he said, "It wasn't me."

Well, since my wife and I had forgotten to take our "stupid pills" that day, we realized that he was not giving us a completely accurate account of the situation. I guess he figured that his best shot to keep from being in trouble was to try and deny the obvious. It didn't work, but he did try.

The truth is that humans of all ages sometimes attempt to deny the obvious in matters that may result in their being viewed in ways that they don't desire. Bigotry is a classic example. Very few want to be labeled as a bigot, regardless of if it is deserved or not. This is especially true in Freemasonry. Freemasonry views itself as a moral and upright Order that takes good men and gives them the tools to make themselves better. But is that goal always completely realized? I believe that if we are honest with ourselves, many of us can recall comments or actions by some Masons that can fairly be defined as bigoted. The goals of Freemasonry do not always succeed with its members.

In the United States, society deemed it acceptable to *own* fellow human beings until the time of the Civil War in the 1860's. Slaves were regularly brought in from Africa to be sold mostly as field workers in the Southern states. But slaves were not limited to field work, they may have been servants inside the homes, or anything that the slave owners wanted. Slaves were considered property. And this could have been in any part of the United States.

Until the time of the Civil War, many U.S. Freemasons were slave owners. The same is true of many U.S. politicians from local city council members all the way up to Presidents of the United States. Slavery was a part of the way of life in this country from its beginning. Then after four years of civil war, it all ended. It was no longer legal in the U.S. for one human being to own another. But how does the human mind fully justify *owning* another human and then all of a sudden switch to the position that such an act is not only illegal but immoral? If it is illegal now because it is immoral, was it immoral in the past? Could they accept that they, as well as their fathers, grandfathers and so on, acted immorally as this new law forced them to examine? Could society turn on a dime, change their moral standards, and accept their guilt for their past immoral acts like flipping a light switch on and off? Could society instantly change like that? The answer is no.

Following the Civil War, slave owners were no longer allowed to own slaves, but most maintained their attitude towards former slaves. It would seem that the only way that one could morally justify owning another human being was to consider the slave as something less than human. Slaves were often considered in the same category as expensive farm equipment. This opinion did not change for former slave owners. They were not going to label themselves, or past family members, as immoral in their actions.

On paper, slavery was outlawed by federal law following the Civil War. Former slaves were now citizens of the United States, but were all citizens equal? Hardly. For the next hundred years, until the 1950's and 60's, Jim Crow laws made it very clear that some citizens were more important than others. Some Jim Crow laws remain even today in stubborn areas. While black men were technically eligible to vote, many to most didn't because of restrictive state laws. Segregation of the races became the law of the land in many areas. The races were divided and where you went and what you did was restricted by your race.

Freemasonry is part of society. Its members come from the towns and areas around the lodges. If society is segregated, then so is Freemasonry. If society is bigoted, then so are the members of Freemasonry — regardless of its teachings. Prior to the desegregation movement and law changes of the 1950's and 60's, no US Grand Lodge viewed Prince Hall Freemasonry as anything but irregular. Prince Hall Freemasonry was created because lodges in the US, by far, were considered "white only." I joined Freemasonry in the mid 1970's, and every single US Grand Lodge officially viewed Prince Hall Freemasonry as "clandestine." It was not until 1989 that the first US Grand Lodge, the Grand Lodge of Connecticut, entered into Fraternal Relations with their Prince Hall counterpart.

False Pride is one of the *Seven Deadly Sins*. We can trace so many failures in humanity to acts of ego and pride. After all, if humans were not affected by this type of pride, why would we need to announce it as a sin to be avoided? But what is this pride? It is arrogance, conceit, superiority, and ego on steroids. Because false pride is a sin, it is by its nature contrary to moral teachings and living. It is wrong. We must recognize it as something to be avoided if we want to live a moral life. Pride and being wrong are also tied together and need each other. One filled with arrogant pride cannot admit to being in error. They embrace errors because of their pride. Lies become truth in their world. A bigot cannot admit that his feelings are wrong because his pride embraces these errors and rejects the concept that he could be wrong. He claims to have pride in his family and will not admit that they could be in any error for how they felt and how they taught him. This type of pride will not change because to change, one must admit that change is needed. In other words, they were wrong, and they won't accept that they could be wrong. When one removes pride from the equation, change takes place.

I remember back in my early days of Masonry. There was a Mason that I knew who was in his late seventies. He was always friendly, but somewhat quiet and reserved. In talking with him, it became clear that he had bigoted feelings.

This was back in the early 1980s. I don't know much about his early years or what happened in his life to give him these bigoted tendencies, but he was not shy about telling anyone his feelings. If you were not white, he didn't think much of you.

The elderly brother was a widower. He had one daughter who lived about twenty-five miles outside of New Orleans in a town called LaPlace. She was married and had several children. I would see the brother at most lodge meetings. I began to notice him becoming even more withdrawn and reserved. He hardly spoke to anyone. I asked him if anything was wrong, and he opened up with me. He said that he and his daughter had a bad argument, and they had not spoken in several months. You could tell that this situation weighed heavily on him. After several more meetings, his attitude completely changed, and he seemed back to his old self. I asked him how things were going with his family situation. He said that everything was fine again, and that he was having dinner at his daughter's house that coming weekend. At the next meeting, I asked him how the dinner went. He said that the dinner was wonderful, but what happened after the dinner was the most traumatic thing that he had ever experienced.

The brother said that he had left his daughter's house about 9:00 o'clock in the evening and began the drive home. No sooner then he had left the house then it started raining. By the time he got to the I-10, the rain was so heavy that he could hardly see. Now, there is an area between LaPlace and New Orleans known as the Bonnet Carre Spillway. It's basically a swamp. It's just a bridge crossing an area filled with water, alligators, snakes, and all the other nasty things that normally live in a swamp. He said that as he was crossing the Spillway, the rain was so heavy that he was having difficulty staying within the lines. He didn't see well at night. Then all of a sudden, he heard a loud noise, and he almost lost control of the car. He had blown a front tire.

The brother was able to pull over, and he got out of the car. He was immediately drenched by the heavy rain. He was badly shaken by the events. He said that the shoulder of the highway was very small, and it was pitch black all around. The only thing that he could see were the lights of the other cars as they sped by him. He was terrified and felt that he would certainly be hit by a car and die in that swamp. I could see in his eyes the fear that he felt from that situation.

The brother said that he knew that the only way that he could come out of this alive was to somehow get help. Soaking wet and very shaken, he went to the front of the car and stood in the light of the headlights so that he could be seen. He signaled for help in a way that Masons do when they feel that their life is in danger. He said that fear for his life guided him to do this. Several cars passed him with no sign of slowing down. Then a car came up fast and apparently seeing him, hit the brakes. The car's brakes squealed, and the car slid to a stop a little way in front of him. It was then that his eyes became wide as he was retelling the story.

He said, "Mike, all four doors of that car flew open, and out came four large black men." He said, "I was terrified. I *knew* they were going to kill me, and I broke. I started crying like a child."

When the men reached him, they said, "Brother! We've just left a degree rehearsal, what's wrong?" The old brother was awfully shaken and confused. All that he could do was point to the tire. He then told me, "Mike, they were Masons! One of them took off his jacket and put it around me. They told me not to worry about anything, that they would take care of everything." He said that he couldn't believe what was happening. "I told them that I appreciated their help and started to get the spare tire out of the trunk. But they wouldn't let me do anything. One of them put his arm around me and told me to go sit in their car out of the rain, and they would take care of the tire." With a look of total amazement, he told me, "Mike, they changed my tire for me in the pouring rain." He said, "All that I had on me was about $40. When they came back, I told them that this was all I had, but I wanted them to have it. Then one of them stopped me cold. He told me that they didn't want anything because this is what Masons are supposed to do." He then said, "Mike, these black men, these black Masons saved my life! That was the most Masonic thing that I have ever seen!" Then he stood there shaking his head and said, "Mike, I have been wrong about these people my whole life. What do I do? I won't live long enough to make the wrong that I have done right."

I'm passing on this story as an example that each one of us has within us the ability to change. The stimulus that causes us to change may vary, but we can change. We do not have to be controlled by pride or anything else. Every one of us can look deep in our hearts and recognize errors that we have made in thought or deed. We are not less because we have made errors, but we will not become better if we do not acknowledge the errors, change, and move to the correct path. Humanity needs to be one. We are all God's children, and He loves us all equally. We need to do the same. We need to look at and judge the internal, not the external.

Bigotry has existed and does exist in the hearts of some Masons. We *can* acknowledge past wrongs, even terrible wrongs, and change our lives — our way of thinking. We can live according to the teachings of Freemasonry. But we need to stop making excuses and do what is needed to be and live as one people. "For God so loved *the world*," not *some* of the world.

The Two Wolves and Three Bad Guys

It's often said that Freemasonry mirrors society. Well, society is clearly divided right now and, frankly, so is Freemasonry. There is a lot of anger around. I'd like in this paper to look at arguments that can divide us. I don't mean specific arguments; I'd like to look at the concept of division, and its possible causes. Maybe if we understand a bit of the *why* to the question, we can move more towards unity.

I often talk with and receive emails from upset Masons telling me about disagreements that they have had with other Masons. What I find most interesting is that when I talk with both sides, each is absolutely certain that their position is completely correct, while the other guy is completely wrong. And frankly, it's not always clear to me who is right and who is wrong. It can be highly subjective.

But let's take the question of who is right and who is wrong and put it on the side for a moment. As a historian, being able to prove something does not always explain the whole situation. We may be certain that something happened, but if we don't understand *why* it happened, then we don't know the whole story. Why is *this guy* wrong? What makes anyone wrong?

There is an old Cherokee parable that I would like to pass on. I'm sure many of you have heard it, but I believe it is helpful to understand this question.

An old Cherokee is teaching his grandson about life. "A fight is going on inside me," he said to the boy. "It is a terrible fight, and it is between two wolves. One is evil — he is anger, envy, sorrow, regret, greed, arrogance, self-pity, guilt, resentment, inferiority, lies, false pride, superiority, and ego."

He continued, "The other is good — he is joy, peace, love, hope, serenity, humility, kindness, benevolence, empathy, generosity, truth, compassion, and faith. The same fight is going on inside you — and inside every other person, too."

The grandson thought about it for a minute and then asked his grandfather, "Which wolf will win?"

The old Cherokee simply replied, "The one you feed."

The two wolves in this Cherokee parable are not unlike the lesson of the three bad guys in the Hiramic legend. The three bad guys did not invade the Temple from the outside. They were part of the workers. It was an inside job. Yes, there was danger outside of the walls of the Temple, but all the trouble that came in that Masonic Legend came from inside the walls.

The lesson is that yes, we can face problems from outside, but so very many of our problems can be traced to decisions that we make and things that we do, all of our own free will. The problems come from within us.

Those three bad guys gave in to the evil wolf inside of them. And these two wolves are inside us all. The good wolf as well as the bad one.

Additionally, we all have free will and the ability to use it. We can do evil just as well as good. It is our choice. It doesn't mean that we are bad people, but we can do wrong, or maybe, think wrong.

We also have the ability to do wrong but view it as doing good. We are good at deceiving ourselves. The choices that are available to us are greater than we might imagine. We can have no problem at all believing any number of scenarios.

Let's look at a math problem. Let's say that one guy says that 3 + 2 = 5. Another replies, "No, you are wrong. 3 + 3 = 5." Well, we know that the second guy is wrong. It's basic math, and it can be proven. But let's not forget free will. The second guy does not have to believe anything that he doesn't want to believe. He may have no credibility at all, but he can still argue. He can fight and demand that he is correct. We do have the ability to accept whatever reality that we want to accept.

But the one who was mathematically correct also has free will. He can also feed whichever wolf he wishes. He can realize that the second guy is just wrong and walk away, or he can continue to argue and fight with him.

Let's look again at math. Let's say that someone says that 3 + 2 = 5. But someone else says that 4 + 1 = 5. Well, neither answer is wrong. They both came to the correct conclusion. They arrived at the answer in different ways, but they both gave the correct answer.

However, they both then insist that *their way* is the *only way*. They will not acknowledge that the other guy might also be correct in his answer. They fight and fight and fight, becoming true enemies. They will now do everything that they can to destroy the other. Why?

They are both feeding the same evil wolf inside of them. They have both allowed false pride, arrogance, ego and anger to control them. You can have the right answer, but still be wrong in your actions.

The Two Wolves and Three Bad Guys

Most arguments that I have seen that break out in Masonry involve opinions of Masonry. I've never seen one involving mathematical problems. One group might believe that the best way to operate Masonry will be by doing *this*. Another group will believe that it is best to do *that*. Neither group wants to destroy Masonry, they just have different ideas as to the best way to operate. Both groups want *their way* accepted as the *best way*.

The truth is that if you have two groups with different ideas of how to make something better, then that can be a very positive situation. If they work together, they can often come up with a third plan that combines the best of the two original plans.

By working together, they do better work than by going it alone. That's Masonry. That's feeding the good wolf.

Masonry teaches us that we are Brothers. Families sometimes fight. 3 + 2 = 5, but so does 4 + 1. Sometimes we have the same goal, but just head there by different paths. There is nothing wrong in that. It's not unMasonic to think differently.

But, when we allow the evil wolf to get hold of us and control our actions, well, *we* become the problem. Two sides can be equally wrong. When minds just can't be changed, walk away. Freemasonry and its teachings come first.

Groups of Masons, lodges, Grand Lodges, or *any* aspect of Masonry is part of Masonry. It is not Masonry itself. If you can't find Masonry here, find it there. But don't be a part of the problem. Don't feed the bad wolf. Let the bad wolf starve.

Vouching for Someone — Yes or No

Recently, I saw a question asked in an online forum about Masons vouching for other Masons. In reading some of the answers, a few gave me some concern. Some were very specific to jurisdictions. So, I would like to talk a little bit about the subject of vouching.

In short, vouching for someone is when you tell a lodge, "Yes, I know this man to be a Freemason." You are giving your word to the lodge that you know of no reason why he should not visit and sit in lodge with everyone. The lodge will usually admit him with no further examination. They know you to be a Mason and take your word that he is a Mason.

The first thing that must be made very clear is that what I've just said is the general US Masonic idea of vouching for another. What has to be kept in mind is that each and every jurisdiction has its own rules and regulations. What is proper and allowed in one jurisdiction might be outlawed in another.

One of the major problems that I have seen in multi-jurisdictional online forms is misinformation. A question will be asked by someone on these forums. Someone else will then come on and with all the "authority" in the world, give out an answer that may be completely correct for his jurisdiction, yet completely wrong in the jurisdiction of the one asking the question. Unsuspecting, and trusting, young Masons will sometimes take incorrect information (for their jurisdiction) back to their lodge.

So, with the very clear warning that what I am saying may or may not apply to your jurisdiction, I'll continue.

Let's look at an example. Let's say that last month you went to lodge "A" and met some brother during the meeting of the lodge. Now, the following month, you are in lodge "B," maybe it's your own lodge, and this brother who you met in lodge last month shows up and wants to visit.

No one else in the lodge knows this brother, and they ask around before the meeting if anyone has sat in lodge with him. Well, you did sit in lodge with him and remember him well. You let the Master or one of the officers know that you have sat in lodge with him.

At the opening of the lodge, they may or may not challenge him. If they do, this would be your cue to stand up and *vouch* for him in lodge. This tells the lodge that you know him to be a Mason. Things would then usually move on, and the lodge would open. That's normally considered how we vouch for someone.

But let's take another scenario. Let's say that you are having lunch somewhere with a Mason. You have sat with him in lodge many times over the years and consider him a personal friend. A man comes up to the table and says hello to your friend. You've never met him before. The Mason you do know immediately shakes his hand and greets him as a longtime friend. Clearly, they know each other. Your friend introduces you and tells you that he belongs to a local lodge. They exchange a few friendly words, and then he leaves.

A month or two later, this friend of your friend shows up at your lodge. Remember, you have never actually sat in lodge with him. All that you know is what your friend told you. So, can you vouch for this man based on your meeting him at that lunch?

In most jurisdictions, the answer is no.

To vouch for someone, *you* would need to have recently and physically sat in lodge with the one for whom you are vouching. Meeting someone at lunch and being told that he belongs to a lodge is usually not enough. This is called second-hand vouching. This is when someone tells you that someone else is a Mason outside a lodge setting. You then vouch for the individual in the lodge.

Again, some jurisdictions may allow second-hand vouching as in this situation.

The difference between the two is the formal setting of a lodge. In order to be able to vouch for someone, you have to have examined him, seeing his current dues card, or sat in lodge with him during that year. The idea is that if you have done one of these two things, you know him to be a current Mason who is not suspended or expelled.

In an informal setting, like a restaurant, dues cards are probably not exchanged and actual current membership can only be assumed. He could have been suspended last year, and you just don't know about it.

Again, different jurisdictions have different rules. You must ask your Worshipful Master, DDGM, or someone in your Grand Lodge.

Another situation that can happen is the question of vouching for someone in absence.

Let's say that you receive a phone call from a member of your lodge telling you that they will not be able to make a meeting that is scheduled for the next night or two. He tells you that a friend of his is coming to the lodge from out of state. He tells you that he knows him to be a Mason and asks you to vouch for him.

This is really the same type of situation as the lunch meeting. Vouching for someone is something that is most usually done in lodge and in person. Someone is challenged in lodge as to their Masonic membership. If you know him to be a Mason, you stand up and vouch for him.

You are giving your word that *you* have sat in lodge with him or examined him. Second-hand vouching leaves the door open for many problems. Unless you have sat in lodge with someone, and done so *this year*, how do you know, for fact, that he was not suspended this very year for NPD? You can't know.

Now, some jurisdictions do allow second-hand vouching. Some absolutely do not allow it. You need to check the laws of your jurisdiction, and this should be a part of every lodge's education program (along with all the private details of vouching).

Now, let's take another situation.

Let's say that last night you attended a meeting of the Scottish Rite, York Rite, or some other body of Masonry. Brother Jones was there as usual. You have seen him in this body many, many other times. He is a regular attender. But, tonight, he shows up at your lodge to visit. You realize that you have never sat in a craft lodge with him. If no one else knows him, can you vouch for this brother?

Well, this is exactly the same as second-hand vouching. Yes, you have sat in another body of Masons with him. And sure, you can't belong to the Scottish Rite or York Rite if you are not a craft lodge Mason, but that does not overcome the problem.

Either *you* have sat in a *craft lodge* with someone, or you have not. Either you follow the rules, or you don't. Again, some jurisdictions do allow second-hand vouching, but some do not. You need to know your laws as this situation could create serious problems. It may feel very awkward to tell someone you always see in other Masonic bodies that you can't vouch for them in a craft lodge. But once again, either you have sat in a craft lodge with someone, or you have not.

Some jurisdictions will not allow the examination of EAs or Fellowcrafts. They must be accompanied and vouched for by Master Masons in order to visit lodges. But again, each jurisdiction has its own rules.

More and more jurisdictions are switching back to allowing business meetings to be held in the EA degree. With education in mind, it has been realized by a number of jurisdictions that there is value to EAs and Fellowcrafts seeing how business is done in lodges.

It cannot be said enough — knowing the rules and regulations of your jurisdiction is indispensable. For officers not to know is inexcusable.

The lodge should be a special place for all Masons. No, the world will not end if someone who should not visit a lodge does so. But if rules and regulations mean something to you, then you should follow them. If you don't know the rules and regulations, then how can you know what is right or what is wrong?

Not knowing the basics of Masonry is how lodges and jurisdictions fall apart. This is one of the reasons why Masonic education is so very important.

Capt. Kirk Goes to Space — Now You Do Something!

As a kid, I remember watching the original *Star Trek* TV show in the mid to late 1960's. It only lasted a few seasons, but then it went into reruns which became more popular than the original series. *Star Trek* movies and numerous spin-off TV shows followed. *Star Trek* turned into a very successful franchise. William Shatner starred in the role of Captain James T. Kirk, commander of the starship *Enterprise*. The acting was, at times, over the top, but it made for an enjoyable show. This was not Shatner's first or last TV role or movie. He played in a popular episode of TV's *The Twilight Zone* and then later stared in TV's *T.J. Hooker* and *Boston Legal*. But it would be fair to say that Shatner's role in *Star Trek* was his most popular. But what has Bill Shatner been up to lately? Well …

On October 13, 2021, actor William Shatner, at 90, became the oldest person to travel into space. It was not a TV show or movie. He actually went into space as a passenger aboard Blue Origin's *New Shepard* spacecraft. Blue Origin is a company owned by Amazon founder Jeff Bezos. Not surprisingly, Shatner drew both praise and criticism for his venture into space (I believe mostly due to his perceived personality). In reading accounts from both those in praise of him and the critics, they all seemed to miss the point. I don't believe that it matters if you think William Shatner is the bravest guy in the world or a fool for his visit to space. The point is that this 90 year-old-man didn't just get up one morning, eat a bowl of oatmeal, and watch game shows on TV all day. This 90-year-old got up, allowed himself to be strapped into a seat in a *spacecraft*, blasted off, and went up into space. Like it or not, think it is crazy or not, this guy *did something* that day! There is a message for all of us here.

Every morning we are given a beautiful gift. No matter how old or young we are, we have the ability to make the most out of each day or do nothing at all. In Masonry, we use the beehive as a symbol of constant accomplishment. We don't look at a beehive and ask the age of the bees. We see the beehive and marvel at how they are all working together towards a goal. They are all doing something and all very busy about it. Their age is irrelevant. They stop when they die. Not long ago, I read about the 2009 Worshipful Master of Hart's Grove Lodge, No. 397 (now Triandria, No. 780) under the jurisdiction of the Grand Lodge of Ohio. Worshipful Brother Harold Potter was 99 years old at the time of his installation. This brother didn't have to take on that job at his age, but he *did something*. He contributed to the whole. He earned his wages.

But "doing something" doesn't mean just letting everyone know how important you are at Masonic meetings. It's disappointing when we see a past Masonic this or that show up at lodges, or other bodies, only to strut around showing off all his honors and awards. What an *important* man this is! But there is often another side to this coin. I also see many real leaders who after attaining every possible honor still serve meals in lodge kitchens, teach young Masons, and participate wherever and however is possible. They are *doing something!*

Improving oneself does not only mean learning but passing on what you have learned. Age means nothing to those who desire to find some way to do something positive. Most Worshipful Brother Robert G. Davis, writes in his book, *The Mason's Words*: "Freemasonry is the pursuit of that which is noble in man." We don't have to go into space to be noble. But inaction does not define noble. We must do something to help others, to help the whole. Potato chips, dip, beer, and a

Netflix movie does not help advance the lessons of Freemasonry. In MWBro. Davis' quote, Freemasonry is the action, the verb, the *doing something*. Freemasonry can't be defined in a title. It must be a lifestyle of growth, of learning, of teaching, of helping, and of doing.

With age comes many aches and pains, but if a 90 year old can go into space and a 99 year old can serve in the East, then we can find some creative way of earning our own wages.

The Theory of Stupidity

Over and over again, we read that Freemasonry takes good men and makes them better. We also read that Freemasonry is a path to enlightenment. In thinking about it, I have to wonder if these two statements mean (or are understood to mean) the same thing. If someone gains enlightenment today, then we can fairly say that they have become "better" than they were yesterday. But if someone is feeling sick and tomorrow, he is feeling "better," does that mean that he has gained enlightenment? No, getting over a cold is *not* the same as becoming enlightened. Sometimes words have deeper meanings than the obvious. We must be careful not to misunderstand.

Merriam-Webster's online dictionary gives us two definitions of the word *enlightened*:

"1: freed from ignorance and misinformation.
... *an enlightened people*
... *an enlightened time*

"2: based on full comprehension of the problems involved.
... *issued an enlightened ruling*" [1]

It would seem that *enlightened* is an antonym of *ignorant* (the state an enlightened person is freed from) or *stupid*. But to be sure, let's see how Merriam-Webster's online dictionary defines "stupid." We see three definitions of "stupid."

"1: not intelligent: having or showing a lack of ability to learn and understand things.
... *She angrily described her boss as a stupid old man.*
... *He had a stupid expression on his face.*
... *I'm not stupid enough to fall for that trick.*

"2: not sensible or logical: foolish
... *Why are you being so stupid?*
... *It was stupid of me to try to hide this from you.*

"3: not able to think normally because you are drunk, tired, etc.
... *Two glasses of wine are enough to make me stupid.*
... *I was stupid with fatigue.*" [2]

The third example would seem to be a temporary state. If you are *stupid* because you are drunk, then it will pass with time. You can sleep to recover from being tired. This example seems to provide little help with our understanding of the original question. But we will come back to it later.

The first example speaks of ignorance. But there is a great difference between one who is ignorant because he does not know something and one who is ignorant because he does not have the capacity to learn. You can be ignorant of who is in the next room, but you will overcome that ignorance by walking into the room and discovering who is there. If you do not have the ability to understand or learn, then this is very different from not yet having learned something.

If the goal of Freemasonry is to enlighten its membership, then it has little to offer one who does not have the ability to learn. If the word unenlightened is understood to mean that the individual is *stupid* in the sense of not being able to learn or grow in any collection of facts or information, then we cannot make this person "better" by this understanding of the word. We cannot offer enlightenment to such individuals unless we were merely mocking them in a callous manner.

In the second definition of the word *stupid*, it speaks of one who is "not sensible or logical: foolish." This is an interesting definition as it does not address the ability to learn. Someone who is foolish or lacking in any common sense can still learn. One lacking common sense can graduate (and many have graduated) from universities earning many different degrees.

These words have enough flexibility in meanings to create situations where some may view the meanings in relationship to

Freemasonry one way, and others see them completely differently. Let's try to look a little deeper.

In the third definition of "stupid," the word can be understood as one who is intoxicated, drunk. Anyone can become drunk by drinking too much alcohol. At this time, another common phrase of Freemasonry needs to be mentioned: "Freemasonry is a peculiar system of morality, veiled in allegory and illustrated by symbols." Going around habitually drunk is often considered immoral in most societies. The old Operatives would quickly dismiss one who showed up to work drunk. Today, if any Mason sits drunk in a lodge at labor, he can reasonably expect to face Masonic discipline, including trial.

If we look at the word *stupid* and use it to mean a state of tiredness or exhaustion from lack of sleep, then we can also look at aspects of our Masonic teachings. The 24 inch-gage is often used in Speculative Masonry as a symbol of time management. We recognize the need for resting our mind and body. The old Operatives were expected to show up at work, ready to work. An Operative who was not in a fit state to work because he was tired would display a disregard for what was necessary to perform his duties. If he was not fit to work, then he was not fit to remain a Fellow of the Craft.

If the goal of Freemasonry is to "get better" or grow and we do so by learning (enlightenment), then clearly one who is *stupid* because he is routinely drunk is unfit. You can't learn while you are drunk. Someone who burns the candle at both ends and is always in a state of exhaustion may also be unfit as his mind may always be somewhere other than where it should be. If he should be paying attention, he may be falling asleep. If given directions, he may ignore or forget them.

If, on the other hand, we define the word *stupid* to mean ignorant, as in simply not knowing something, well, that is a different story. If one is basically a good and moral person, has the capacity to learn (and seeks to grow in knowledge), then they may well be a good candidate for Freemasonry. We expect that one coming into Freemasonry to be ignorant of its teachings. I believe that this is the intention and understanding of the phrases.

But take a closer look at one of the other definitions of *stupid* — the definition: "not sensible or logical: foolish." Let's look at this definition and how it may be understood and apply to Freemasonry.

I believe that we may often ignore this alarming definition of stupid. In fact, it may be a case of "hidden in plain sight" as much has been written about it. In this understanding of the word, one is lacking common sense and logic. As such, they can learn many facts and figures and, on the surface, seem quite intelligent, but they often fail at many common tasks. They do not think of problems that may be created by their actions. They do not think out situations. They may seem and act clearly *stupid*. In doing things that they find acceptable; they can be dangerous to themselves and others. These types are also often unfit.

Let me give you a simple example of one lacking common sense. Let's say that a group of friends gathered at a friend's house a few days before a large storm was set to hit. A group of them were sleeping in the living room on cots, sleeping bags, and such. It was in the middle of the night when one friend woke up to see another sitting up reading from his cell phone. He asked his friend, "What's wrong?"

His friend answered, "Just can't sleep." Not knowing the time, but seeing his friend looking right at his cell phone, he asked, "What time is it?" Instead of looking at his phone to see the time, the friend got up and walked over to the wall light switch. He then flipped on the overhead lights so that he could see the clock hanging on the wall. Of course, everyone in the room woke up yelling.

The one who turned on the lights displayed a great lack of common sense (and consideration). Let's try to look at his thought process and actions. The man had a problem; he was asked the time, and he did not know the time. To solve his problem, he needed to find out the time. To tell the time, you can look at a clock — like the one that he knew was on the wall. He couldn't do that because it was dark. So, what did he do to solve all his problems? He gets up and turns on the light in the room so that he can look at the clock, learn the time, and tell his friend the time. He acted *stupid*. By not considering everyone in the room sleeping, he created a problem for everyone, including himself.

The man did not stop to think that by turning on the lights, he would suddenly startle and wake everyone in the room. He didn't think. He did not think out the consequences of his actions nor alternatives that he might have done to accomplish his goal and not disturb everyone. He just acted with the first thing that came to his mind that he knew would solve his problem. He just did not stop to think about if it was the best or only way to solve his problem.

This lack of common sense — stupidity — (in its countless forms) has, throughout history, been the cause of more turmoil, and suffering, than can be counted. We see acts of stupidity every day. Some are minor acts, some monumental. Albert Einstein is quoted as saying, "Two things are infinite: the universe and human stupidity; and

The Theory of Stupidity

I'm not sure about the universe." But this type of stupidity sometimes has dire consequences.

Dietrich Bonhoeffer (1906-1945) was a German minister, author, and anti-Nazi dissident. Bonhoeffer was arrested and hung by the Nazi's after being accused of playing a role in an assassination plot against Adolf Hitler. Bonhoeffer wrote extensively on how a whole country could be so taken in by someone like Hitler. Bonhoeffer wrote his "Theory of Stupidity" in a series of letters, expounding on the dangers of not only Hitler, but those who would follow him. His thoughts are important.

> "Stupidity is a more dangerous enemy of the good than malice. One may protest against evil; it can be exposed and, if need be, prevented by use of force. Evil always carries within itself the germ of its own subversion in that it leaves behind in human beings at least a sense of unease. Against stupidity we are defenseless. Neither protests nor the use of force accomplish anything here; reasons fall on deaf ears; facts that contradict one's prejudgment simply need not be believed — in such moments the stupid person even becomes critical — and when facts are irrefutable they are just pushed aside as inconsequential, as incidental. In all this the stupid person, in contrast to the malicious one, is utterly self-satisfied and, being easily irritated, becomes dangerous by going on the attack. For that reason, greater caution is called for than with a malicious one. Never again will we try to persuade the stupid person with reasons, for it is senseless and dangerous.

"If we want to know how to get the better of stupidity, we must seek to understand its nature. This much is certain, that it is in essence not an intellectual defect but a human one. There are human beings who are of remarkably agile intellect yet stupid, and others who are intellectually quite dull yet anything but stupid. We discover this to our surprise in particular situations. The impression one gains is not so much that stupidity is a congenital defect, but that, under certain circumstances, people are made stupid or that they allow this to happen to them. We note further that people who have isolated themselves from others or who live in solitude manifest this defect less frequently than individuals or groups of people inclined or condemned to sociability. And so it would seem that stupidity is perhaps less a psychological than a sociological problem. It is a particular form of the impact of historical circumstances on human beings, a psychological concomitant of certain external conditions. Upon closer observation, it becomes apparent that every strong upsurge of power in the public sphere, be it of a political or of a religious nature, infects a large part of humankind with stupidity. It would even seem that this is virtually a sociological-psychological law. The power of the one needs the stupidity of the other. The process at work here is not that particular human capacities, for instance, the intellect, suddenly atrophy or fail. Instead, it seems that under the overwhelming impact of rising power, humans are deprived of their inner independence, and, more or less consciously, give up establishing an autonomous position toward the emerging circumstances. The fact that the stupid person is often stubborn must not blind us to the fact that he is not independent. In conversation with him, one virtually feels that one is dealing not at all with a person, but with slogans, catchwords and the like that have taken possession of him. He is under a spell, blinded, misused, and abused in his very being. Having thus become a mindless tool, the stupid person will also be capable of any evil and at the same time incapable of seeing that it is evil. This is where the danger of diabolical misuse lurks, for it is this that can once and for all destroy human beings.

"Yet at this very point it becomes quite clear that only an act of liberation, not instruction, can overcome stupidity. Here we must come to terms with the fact that in most cases a genuine internal liberation becomes possible only when external liberation has preceded it. Until then we must abandon all attempts to convince the stupid person. This state of affairs explains why in such circumstances our attempts to know what 'the people' really think are in vain and why, under these circumstances, this question is so irrelevant for the person who is thinking and acting responsibly. The word of the Bible that the fear of God is the beginning of wisdom declares that the internal liberation of human beings to live the responsible life before God is the only genuine way to overcome stupidity.

"But these thoughts about stupidity also offer consolation in that they utterly forbid us to consider the majority of people to be stupid in every circumstance. It really will depend on whether those in

> power expect more from people's stupidity than from their inner independence and wisdom."[3]

In Bonhoeffer's powerful and insightful words, he said that against stupidity we are "defenseless." I disagree with him in that thought. The world has Freemasonry. The world has paths to enlightenment. If we look at stupidity from within the world and language of Freemasonry, then a stupid person can be seen as one who is without Light — and he is unfit to find it while in that state. In Freemasonry, our teachings lead us from the darkness (stupidity) to the Light (state of enlightenment). Light (enlightenment) cannot be given to us in any manner — not as a degree, honor, office, or prize. We, and we alone, must discover it. We must find it through work, study, and understanding the teachings that we are offered in Freemasonry. I don't mean the memorization of a series of unexplained words; I mean through the understanding of what our words, symbols, and lessons mean.

We are *not* just another club for the enjoyment and entertainment of our members. Our goal is *not* to raise a few dollars for those in need. We are *not* to blindly and stupidly bow at the feet of our leaders to feed their egos. Our purpose is and always has been to fight stupidity and lift up not only our members, but the world out of the darkness of stupidity and into the Light of a better world.

Look close at our lessons. All that we teach, all that we offer in clear language or by means of symbolism is designed to liberate the stupid person, the individual, from his state of stupidity. Freemasonry gives him the "tools" to accomplish this work. Our lessons are to bring Light (education of a better way of life) to those in need of it (those under the influence of stupidity). We are taught early on that our only concern is the human — the stripped down, void of worldly riches and external trappings, human being. We are taught to care about and help each other. It is not for the individual, the student, or candidate to tell Freemasonry the nature of stupidity. They are to listen and learn. It is for those with the desire to find Light to open their minds and hearts and allow the teachings of Freemasonry to reach into them.

Those who come to Freemasonry with anything but a humble, seeking heart will find nothing but a collection of silly rituals and empty business meetings. They will not find the true Light. They will remain (in coarse terms) stupid. But for those who come to Masonry with the determined desire to grow and learn, they can climb out of the dark hole of ignorance to find the true Light, the true gold of Freemasonry. Every initiate must come of his own free-will and accord. They must come with a desire to become more than they are, better than they are. They must be open to change, desire it, and be ready to grow (and often fight) through change. Only then can one move from the darkness (by whatever name you call it — ignorance, blindness, stupidity, etc.) become a Freemason, and earn his true wages.

NOTES:

1. https://www.merriam-webster.com/dictionary/enlightened.
2. https://www.merriam-webster.com/dictionary/stupid
3. Dietrich Bonhoeffer, *'After Ten Years' in Letters and Papers from Prison* (Dietrich Bonhoeffer Works/English, vol. 8) Minneapolis, MN: Fortress Press, 2010

The Importance of Quality Leadership

In Masonry we speak of "meeting on the level." It is an essential element of who we are as Freemasons. But, while it has profound symbolic meaning in Masonry, it is a phrase that can be misunderstood and one that can create problems. "Meeting on the level" does not mean that we all have equal abilities, knowledge, or experience.

For the most part, candidates come to us with little knowledge of who or what we are. Yes, some have read books on Freemasonry or watched Masonic themed movies, but few know the organization of Freemasonry. They don't know, nor should they know, how we operate or our place in the world. It is our job to teach the new Mason. Just as the old Operatives instructed their new Apprentices, so must we provide all necessary education to our new members. But, when we don't, what happens?

More than a few times, I have seen Masons who were wholly unqualified advance to leadership positions in all bodies of Masonry. They may be as nice and friendly as the day is long, but they are simply unqualified for their position. They may lack knowledge of our rituals, philosophy, or customs — or they may know none of it. They may have moved into an office because there was a need; they were there; and they were felt by others to be "acceptable." But there is more to the "why" of this story.

Somewhere along the way, some of us embraced an idea that the presiding officer of any Masonic body is a mere figurehead. The real work is felt to come from the secretary. It is the secretary who does all the actual work. Because secretaries usually hold office more than a year, they have gained skills by necessity (at least, hopefully). The "leader" is there mostly to fill a constitutionally mandated slot. I understand the logic behind such an idea. Elections are *yearly*, and we simply do not have enough qualified individuals to fill all the slots year after year. Our choice has been to fall apart or make compromises that may *seem* to solve the problem. The reality is, however, that this solution turns our foundation from stone to sand.

When a lodge *meets on the level*, everyone, including the Worshipful Master (and also the Grand Master if he is present) physically moves so that all are standing on the same level. Certainly, a Worshipful Master has more authority than the rest of the members of a lodge. The Grand Master has even more authority. But what does "authority" mean? More than a few times, I have seen Worshipful Masters unable to answer even simple questions without turning to the secretary or an inner circle of Past Masters for guidance. What "authority" can someone who is unqualified be allowed to possess?

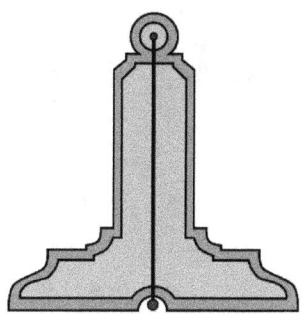

The practice of "meeting on the level" comes from the days of the old Operative Masons. It was to show that all Freemasons were of the same class system. The Master of the Works was not a superior human being because of the job that he performed. Yes, the duties of the Master of the Works were far more demanding and required far more skill than the work of a stone cutter. Jobs were given to the ones most qualified, not ones who were in the "right group" or because no one else was available. They were *all* highly trained, and each did their own skilled job. Their team effort produced results worthy of awe. If *any* of them did not perform their assigned duties, then the whole effort could result in failure. A qualified leader elevates the whole Masonic organization. An unqualified one, or one being held up by others, reduces the organization to club status. Yes, a great leader has inborn abilities which cannot be taught. But a skilled leader is one who has taken the time to learn what is necessary to preside in a manner that elevates, not diminishes. A lodge is to instruct, and the student is to learn. When one or both do not take place, failure is the result.

If what we do means nothing, then we can survive with figureheads as our leaders. But if we are to build and do the work that we were created to do, then we need *all* of our workers to be skilled in their jobs — the ones from least to most rank. All become skilled through Masonic education.

A Whole Wide World of Masonic Memories

I was recently asked a question by a young Mason that gave me considerable cause to stop and think. And after thinking about the answer for a while, I felt pretty good. I'd like to share some of this with you.

The Mason asked me if I could tell him some of my favorite memories of Freemasonry. This would include people and events. I had to stop for a moment, as it put me in a very different frame of mind.

Most of the time, I am asked historical questions about the Scottish Rite or Masonry in general. I also hear from young Masons telling me of how frustrated they are in their Masonic experience. But this question forced me to go back in my memories to times that were truly very pleasant. I do remember some very good Masons — friends and good times.

Among the Masons who I remember the most, was one Mason who was really one of my Masonic role models. He has long gone to his reward. I well remember many afternoons sitting in the Masonic Temple Building in New Orleans, going over the Masonic memory work and listening to his Masonic stories. His name was Irl Fergerson, and he was the Chairman of the Permanent Committee on Work of the Grand Lodge of Louisiana. He was the first chairman following the change of that committee from a do-nothing to do-something committee. He did more for Louisiana Freemasonry than most realize. He also knew the Masonic ritual inside and out.

There was a kindness, humility, and wisdom in that Brother that I will never forget. Yea, just thinking about sitting up there talking with him brings back some very, very good memories.

I also remember another Mason who helped form my view of the Scottish Rite. He has also long gone to his reward. I would spend considerable time in his law office right across the street from the Scottish Rite Valley of New Orleans on Carondelet Street. His name was P. Fred Siegel. And I know that these names mean nothing to most everyone, but I just wanted to say them again. I owe them a lot.

Bro. Fred became the Treasurer of the New Orleans Scottish Rite Valley and held every office there including the presiding officer of the Grand Consistory of Louisiana. We would talk a great deal of the philosophy of the Scottish Rite. His mind was shaped by the law, and I was fascinated by how he approached problems. He was always very clear and logical in what he viewed as right and wrong. I very much enjoyed talking about Masonry with him.

I also remember my very early days of Masonry. I remember the brothers who took me around as an EA to the lodges having EA degrees so that I could see the degrees for myself. It's hard to do this today because so few degrees are being conferred. But these weekly visits to lodges to see the degrees helped me a great deal. It also created a strong bond with these brothers, and they made me see how much Masonry can mean when put into action. It was very good and enjoyable times.

I know the old saying, "that was then, and this is now," so let's look at today. Yes, Masonry and society are different today than 40 plus years ago. But still, every morning the sun rises, and we have a new day to do whatever we want. We can do positive things, things that hurt others, or we can do nothing at all. Each day is a blank page.

For some, I believe that they feel as if they never had a chance to enjoy their Masonic "childhood." All of a sudden, they became the "senior" Masons in their lodge, and it feels like they never had a chance to benefit from being the new guy. They may have been thrown into office as soon as they joined. They may never have had the opportunity to watch their own Masonic leaders in action, and now others look to *them* for the answers to questions that no one ever answered for them. Masonry may not feel "fun" at all.

The brother who asked me this question was one who never really experienced his own Masonic childhood. He, like so many other young Masons, feels that they have missed something. It's probably true. Many have missed much. There is much that many were never taught.

But stop and think for a moment. It's not Masonry's fault if your lodge had few or no real teachers who knew the ritual or philosophy of Freemasonry to teach you. You can't expect someone to give you what they never possessed. Getting upset with them and arguing with them about what you should have but may not have received only generates memories that no one needs.

But there is another good memory that I have in Masonry that tops all the others. It's remembering when some young Mason tells me that the reason why he joined the Scottish Rite or Masonry itself is because of something that I wrote or said. *I promise you* that there is no better reward, or honor, or memory as when some young brother says something like that.

That's the memory that I want for you. And the only way for you to get these memories is to stop worrying about what others haven't or can't give you and go out and do the work to learn Masonry yourself. Yes, I had Masons who helped me in my early days, but they did not teach me the things in Masonic history that I discovered on my own. I did that work myself.

We learn and then we teach. By passing on what you have learned, you will be doing more than you have any idea. Sure, it's always easier when there is someone right there who can answer questions for you, but we need to work with what we have. Sometimes either we do the work, or it does not get done.

There are many good, quality sources where we can find the answers to our questions. We just need to do it. We *can* learn Freemasonry. We can pick up where others left off and do the work that others maybe should have done.

Join, learn, and teach.

Don't worry if there is a lack of teachers around you. Seek out the light, and you will find it. Learn, study, and then share the teachings. Don't make excuses. Don't argue with others, and don't lose faith in Masonry if there is a lack of Masonry in others. Maybe they are just waiting for a teacher like you.

The Rewards and Risks of Masonic Education

I'D like to talk about what is easily the most common email that I receive. It will be from a Mason, usually a young Mason who is disappointed about some aspect of his lodge, or his valley, or his chapter, or, really, any Masonic body. Many times, they seem totally disillusioned as they viewed Freemasonry one way before joining, but now find it, after they have joined, to be something completely different. The particulars vary from case to case, but they are all very unhappy, disappointed, and unsure of what to do next.

In one email I received recently, the brother said that he feels trapped. He studied about Freemasonry before he joined, but after joining he found it to be, in his words, "an old men's social and charity club." They were nice guys, but this was not at all the organization that he wanted to join or believed that he was joining.

He thought, at first, that he was just wrong about the nature of Freemasonry. In fact, the members of his lodge even told him that the problem was that he should not have read anything about Freemasonry before he joined. Maybe, or so he thought, they were right. But then he started reading things from other Masons online in various places that were exactly in line with what he originally believed of Masonry. Why wasn't *this* the Masonry that was practiced in his lodge?

The young Mason did try to change things in his lodge. He wanted to try and improve the Masonic experience, but he hit a brick wall. No one enjoyed the lectures that he tried to give. He had an idea for group book reviews of various Masonic books. No one showed any interest. No one liked group discussions in lodge on Masonic symbolism, history, or anything else having to do with Freemasonry. No one was, at all, interested in changing anything about their routine of opening, minutes, bills, event planning, and closing. *He* began to be viewed as the problem. He lost interest and attended fewer and fewer meetings.

Because the young brother began to attend fewer meetings, he was criticized for not supporting his lodge. He felt guilty and tried again to be active. But, still, there was nothing there in the lodge for him. The same old problems existed. He tried to create programs and develop innovative ideas, but nothing he did changed anything except his reputation. He became known as the troublemaker. He wasn't part of *the team*. He didn't seem to care about them, or what they wanted. No matter what he did, he was disappointing someone. He was different. He was criticized when he attended. He was criticized when he did not attend. And nothing that he did could change anything. What was he to do?

This was the same theme over and over in email after email from so many different Masons. There were profound feelings of hopelessness, disappointment, and frustration, and I mean about Freemasonry!

These were sincere Masons who clearly deeply cared about Freemasonry. What are we doing to these young Masons? What the hell is going on?

I'd like to offer something to think about that has been around for several thousand years. It could be of some help.

There was this philosopher by the name of Plato. He wrote many things on human nature and our desire to understand life and all aspects of it. He wrote something that he called the *Allegory of the Cave*.

Plato said that he wrote the *Allegory of the Cave*, "To compare the effect of education and the lack of it on our nature." I'd like to look a bit at this allegory.

Plato tells us that once there was this dark and damp cave way up in the mountains where a handful of prisoners had spent their entire life chained together. They had never been outside the cave and had no life experience of not being chained together there.

They sat facing a blank stone wall. The chains prevented them from even turning around to see behind them. This limited existence in the dark cave was all that they had ever known since birth.

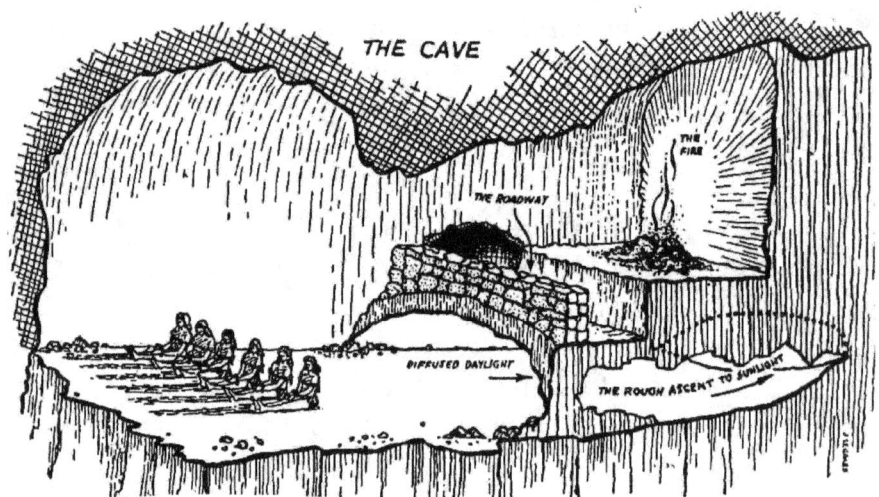

Behind them, and unseen by them, was a raised walkway leading into and then out of the cave. Travelers often walked through the cave, or they came in wagons, leading animals of all sorts and carrying tools, vessels of water, and other things.

Beyond and above this walkway was a large, flattened area near the back wall of the cave. A large fire was always kept burning in this area to give light to the people walking by. But while the prisoners could never see the people or animals walking behind them, the light did create shadows on the wall in front of them.

The prisoners saw only the shadows of everyone and everything that passed through on the roadway. Since birth, they grew up seeing only these shadows passing on the wall in front of them and hearing the muffled voices of people. Never had they seen or known anything else.

Over time, they began to view the shadows as real. They studied the shadows on the walls and believed that if they could understand the shadows, they could understand life. They didn't realize that what they were looking at was only phantoms — a distorted reflection of reality.

The prisoners talked often about the various shadows and took immense pride in their ability to quickly identify images that they saw. This was how they lived, and they had no reason to believe that the world or life was anything other than shadows on a wall.

Now, a day came when one of the prisoners broke free and escaped. He managed to climb out of the cave and made his way to the outside world. When he reached outside, he was blinded by the bright sunlight. He couldn't see anything. But, in time his eyes began to adjust, and he began to see the outside world. He was in awe.

The prisoner began to see the true forms of all the people and things that he had only known before as shadows. He began to see all the colors in the world and the true shapes and nature of all things. He was overjoyed at this new knowledge. All that he had been denied since birth was now made clear.

Out of a feeling of compassion, the prisoner had to run back to the cave to share the truth about the world to his friends. He wanted to help them as he knew that they were in a state of confusion and error as to the true nature of the world.

The prisoner made his way back into the cave, but it was difficult as his eyes had already adjusted to the outside light. The sudden darkness of the cave blinded him. He stumbled down into the cave to where his friends were located.

He made his way to his friends, blinded, stumbling around, but very excited. Seeing him stumbling around and hardly able to see, his friends believed that he had somehow injured himself in his attempt to leave.

The man, out of breath and shaken, told them that the world was nothing at all like they believed. He told them that everything that they believed to be reality was wrong. He told them of the true nature of the sun, the trees, the animals, and all that they had only known as shadows.

The prisoners were in shock. They were being given information that was outside of everything that they had ever known in their existence. And the one giving them all of this incredible information could clearly not see well. He could hardly see the shadows on the wall. The shadows that they could see so well.

They dismissed everything that he said, believing that he was only trying to upset or make fun of them with his falsehoods. They grew increasingly angry at all that he was saying. Finally, they told him that if they could, they would kill him if he kept up trying to make fun of them with his lies. They screamed at him to leave them alone.

Plato explained that the allegory of the cave is the story of all enlightened people. The prisoners in the cave are those who are without enlightenment, lost in a confusion of errors. They are blind to the actual reality of the world. The alienation of the former prisoner returning to them with the truth, is what can be expected for all those who bring truth to those who are not ready to hear it.

For Plato, so many of us live our lives only in the shadows, because for those without a knowledge of the truth, the shadows are accepted as the truth.

Many of the things that we hold of value, such as fame, power, rank, riches are closer to the shadows than we might imagine. They are for the most part, illusions of reality — just as the prisoners saw only the illusions of the reality of all life from the shadows of the cave.

But because everyone around us tells us that the shadows are real, we believe them. We are being taken in by our own lack of knowledge and the appearance of knowledge by others. It's not really our fault, as we were taken in early on, and none of us ever *wanted* to be in that "cave." It is just that this is where we happened to begin our experiences.

But if, like the freed prisoner in the story, you bluntly tell others that they are wrong and that they don't know the truth, you risk a quick backlash of anger and offense. Your intentions will be questioned, and you will be seen as one who only seeks to create problems.

Do you see the parallel to Freemasonry's education problem?

Plato explained that the only way to bring truth to those who are blind to the truth is by a slow process of education. You must not try to force education on anyone. You must not challenge the life experience of anyone or bluntly tell them that they are wrong.

In Masonry, it means that those who have spent the last ten, twenty, thirty or more years in "club Masonry," may truly and honestly believe that what they know is actual Freemasonry. It is all that they have ever known, and they may have spent enough time in this type of shadow Masonry to have risen in rank and authority.

The only way to help Masons in such a situation is to make actual Masonic education available to them in small doses and with a clear attitude of modesty. One method is to ask for the help of one of the leaders in your lodge or other bodies. Let them know that their rank and many years of experience is needed by you to assure a quality program.

Present ideas for education and solicit advice from senior members. Then together investigate the answers. Many times, these Masons will be very confident, or really, overconfident, and tell you that the answers to your questions are really very simple, and everyone already knows all of the answers. You must be very patient with this sort of bravado. It is a fact that while Freemasonry teaches the suppression of ego, many at all levels have an abundance of it. Don't fight it.

To challenge individuals who honestly believe that they are right and who often have fragile egos along with overconfident self-opinions, can bring about hasty angry and hostile reactions. You must be very patient and willing to go over the same questions many times.

It is best to not challenge, but question in a manner to seek clarification and not correction. It may require many meetings and an abundance of patience. Use noted Masonic figures or books in your questioning. You can say, "Albert Mackey wrote this ..." or "I read this in this book..." and then ask them, "What does it mean?"

The sources that you are citing will be the correction that the one that you are dealing with needs. By presenting it as clarification, it allows them to rethink the situation themselves and reach a change of opinion on their own rather than having the correction forced on them by you. It preserves their ego and avoids conflict.

I know that this is really handling these leaders, but if the greater good is desired, then many times we do need to swallow our own pride. The goal is to be of real service, not to feed our own egos. There is, of course, the point of no return. And this is one of the most difficult aspects of Masonic education.

Plato believed that ignorance is a place from where we all start off. It's not our fault, but it is simply how we begin. In far too many lodges, the teachings of Freemasonry have long existed in the archives of the lodges, but they are like an exercise bike in a home that is unused. It's there, but if we don't use it, it is just a room decoration.

Many Masons, many good Masons, have lived their entire lives in Masonry never learning any of the teachings of

Freemasonry. Generations of Masons lived and died with their Freemasonry being little more than a charity club. There is nothing that we can do about that or the past.

There is also nothing that we can do about the fact that we have only a finite number of hours on Earth to do whatever good we choose to do. We must realize that if we spend all of our time helping one Mason or one lodge doggedly stuck in the cave mentality — the club mentality — then we simply may not succeed and may fail to help others who can be helped.

It is a horrible position for any caring person, but in wartime or disaster medical practice, it is known as triage. It's when you have to evaluate the situation and know who to help first. To choose wrong may mean that you end up helping no one. No matter how much it may tear you up inside, you must know when it's time to walk away.

"Freemasonry is a system of morality, veiled in allegory, and illustrated by symbols." Most all Masons have read or heard this. Many don't understand it. Those who have made their way out of the cave of ignorance have a responsibility and duty to the teachings in which they have found light.

You must try to help others find the light. But you must be aware that there is always a danger. There is a danger that your efforts will not only *not* be appreciated by some, but you may also be criticized and even attacked for your efforts. You could be ostracized, shunned, and spoken about in the most unfriendly terms by some. You may be seen as the source of all problems and nothing in the way of a genuine Mason. I promise you, that's OK. Let nothing stand in the way of your helping others.

Don't let words or actions sway you from doing what you know is right. Your job is not to forever placate the ones self-imprisoned in the cave — the ones who refuse to believe anything but that the shadows are the truth of the world. Your job is to be a Freemason. Your job is to share the Light however, wherever, and whenever you can. If doors close to you, then find new doors. Never stop reaching out your hand to help.

In times of war, things do not always go well. True heroes may die. Life does not guarantee happy endings. Doing all that you can, in every way that you can, may well result in your being viewed as no more than a troublemaker by those who once called you brother. None of that matters. Freemasonry is what matters.

Keep in the Light. Share the Light.

About The Author

Michael R. Poll (1954 - present) is the owner of Cornerstone Book Publishers and former editor of the *Journal of The Masonic Society*. He is a Fellow and Past President of The Masonic Society, a Fellow of the Philalethes Society, a Fellow of the Maine Lodge of Research, Member of the Society of Blue Friars, and Full Member of the Texas Lodge of Research.

A New York Times Bestselling writer and publisher, he is a prolific writer, editor, and publisher of Masonic and esoteric books. He is also the host of the YouTube channel "New Orleans Scottish Rite College."

As time permits, he travels and speaks on the history of Freemasonry, with a particular focus on the early history of the Scottish Rite.

He was born in New Orleans, LA and lives a peaceful life with his wife and two sons.

Thank you for buying this Cornerstone book!

For over 25 years now, we've tried to provide the
Masonic community with quality books on
Masonic education, philosophy, and general interest.
Your support means everything to us and
keeps us afloat. Cornerstone is by no means a large
company. We are a small family-owned publishing house
that depends on your support.

Please visit our website and have a look at the
many books we offer as well as the different
categories of books.

If your lodge, Grand Lodge, research lodge, book
club, or other body would like to have quality
Cornerstone books to sell or distribute, write us. We
can give you outstanding books, prices, and service.

Thanks again!

Cornerstone Book Publishers
1cornerstonebooks@gmail.com
http://cornerstonepublishers.com

More Masonic Books from Cornerstone

The Particular Nature of Freemasons
by Michael R. Poll
6x9 Softcover 156 pages
ISBN 9781613423462

A Lodge at Labor
Freemasons and Masonry Today
by Michael R. Poll
6x9 Softcover 180 pages
ISBN 1613421834

The Scottish Rite Papers
A Study of the Troubled History of the Louisiana and US Scottish Rite in the Early to Mid-1800s
by Michael R. Poll
6x9 Softcover 240 pages
ISBN 9781613423448

Measured Expectations
The Challenges of Today's Freemasonry
by Michael R. Poll
6×9 Softcover 180 pages
ISBN: 9781613422946

Seeking Light
The Esoteric Heart of Freemasonry
by Michael R. Poll
6×9 Softcover 156 pages
ISBN: 1613422571

Cornerstone Book Publishers
www.cornerstonepublishers.com

More Masonic Books from Cornerstone

A Masonic Evolution
The New World of Freemasonry
by Michael R. Poll
6x9 Softcover 176 pages
ISBN 9781613423158

10,000 Famous Freemasons
4 Vol. Softcover Edition
by William Denslow
Foreword by Harry S. Truman
Cornerstone Foreword by Michael R. Poll
8.5 x 11, Softcover 2 Volumes 1,515 pages
ISBN 1887560319

The Freemason's Monitor
by Thomas Smith Webb
6×9 Softcover 316 pages
ISBN: 1613422717

An Encyclopedia of Freemasonry
by Albert Mackey
Revised by William J. Hughan and Edward L. Hawkins
Foreword by Michael R. Poll
8.5 x 11, Softcover 2 Volumes 960 pages
ISBN 1613422520

Robert's Rules of Order: Masonic Edition
Revised by Michael R. Poll
6×9 Softcover 212 pages
ISBN: 1613422318

Cornerstone Book Publishers
www.cornerstonepublishers.com

More Masonic Books from Cornerstone

The Freemasons Key
A Study of Masonic Symbolism
Edited by Michael R. Poll
6 x 9 Softcover 244 pages
ISBN: 1887560971

**The Ancient and Accepted Scottish Rite
in Thirty-Three Degrees**
by Robert B. Folger
Introduction by Michael R. Poll
ISBN: 1934935883

10,000 Famous Freemasons
4 Vol. Softcover Edition
by William Denslow
Foreword by Harry S. Truman
Cornerstone Foreword by Michael R. Poll
8.5 x 11, Softcover 2 Volumes 1,515 pages
ISBN 1887560319

A.E. Waite: Words From a Masonic Mystic
Edited by Michael R. Poll
Foreword by Joseph Fort Newton
6 x 9 Softcover 168 pages
ISBN: 1887560734

Masonic Words and Phrases
Edited by Michael R. Poll
6 x 9 Softcover 116 pages
ISBN: 1887560114

Cornerstone Book Publishers
www.cornerstonepublishers.com

www.ingramcontent.com/pod-product-compliance
Lightning Source LLC
Chambersburg PA
CBHW050027130526
44590CB00042B/2000